Strange
PHENOMENA

Strange
PHENOMENA

Peter Henshaw

CHARTWELL
BOOKS, INC.

Published in 2008 by
CHARTWELL BOOKS, INC.
A division of BOOK SALES, INC.
114 Northfield Avenue
Edison, New Jersey 08837
USA

**Copyright © 2008 Regency
House Publishing Limited**
Niall House
24–26 Boulton Road
Stevenage, Hertfordshire
SG1 4QX, UK

For all editorial enquiries, please contact
Regency House Publishing at
www.regencyhousepublishing.com

ISBN-13: 978-0-7858-2401-5

ISBN-10: 0-7858-2401-4

Printed in China

CONTENTS

MYSTERY &
IMAGINATION

Fairies

Crowd Phenomena

Ley Lines

Crop Circles

CHAPTER ONE
MYSTERY & IMAGINATION

FAIRIES

Belief in fairies, elementals, or nature spirits with magical powers, is a recurrent theme in many cultures, and is especially strong within the Celtic fringes of the British Isles and Europe, having spread with colonization, where it still prevails in the Appalachians,

The Wind -Flower Fairy.

Ozarks, and in other such remote areas of America. Such creatures are almost universally seen as diminutive human beings, and only seem to appear in rural settings. The Victorian idea of fairies was of gay (in the old sense of the word) little folk, sitting on toadstools and dancing together in a

FAR LEFT: The Windflower Fairy, from C.M. Barker's Spring Songs with Music, *published circa 1920.*

ABOVE: Naturally occurring in nature but seen by some as a 'fairy' ring. W.B. Yeats wrote: '...the fairies dance in a place apart, Shaking their milk-white feet in a ring,...'.

fairy ring. They are most usually discovered at their revels by innocent children, but vanish from sight when adults or sceptics appear on the scene. But alongside these charming tales of innocent fun there are intimations of more malevolent beings, fond of stealing human children and leaving fairy changelings in their place. Much of the folklore surrounding these

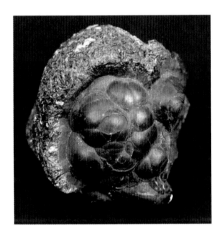

creatures describes ways of protecting oneself from their malice, by using such magical charms as herbs, cold iron (which they abhor), and by never encroaching onto their territory.

During the 16th and 17th centuries, the activities for good and evil of fairies and witches became somewhat blurred and disbelief in both

had become widespread by the late 19th century. A farmer, living on the Isle of Man at that time, believed it had become difficult to see fairies because people had become too occupied with other things, and there's certainly something about the modern pace of life which precludes taking one's time

BELOW LEFT: Cold iron, a powerful protection against malevolent beings.

BELOW: It is claimed that fairies were seen on one of Hoy's towering clifftops. Hoy is part of the Orkney Islands group, located in Britain's far north.

to stand and stare and allowing the little folk to come in.

Sightings of fairies, nonetheless, continued into the 20th century. W.E. Thorner spent two years on the isolated island of Hoy, in the Orkneys, during the Second World War, later writing of his experience when struggling along a clifftop on a wild and windy day: 'I was amazed to see that I had the company of what appeared to be a dozen or more 'wild men' dancing about, to and fro…These creatures were small in stature, but they did not have long noses nor did they appear kindly in demeanour. They possessed round faces, sallow in complexion, with long, dark, bedraggled hair. As they danced about, seeming to throw themselves off the cliff edge, I felt that I was witness to some ritual dance of primitive men.'

But fairies were seen as anything but primitive when two sisters in

LEFT: Doon Hill, in Aberfoyle, Scotland, is the fairy mound within which Robert Kirk is said to have been imprisoned after he collapsed and died in 1692, while on his daily stroll up the hill.

OPPOSITE: Iceland, where over half the population are said to believe in fairies.

Cornwall reported having seen a little white-bearded man in a pointed red hat, driving a miniature car around their lawn; while in Hertford, north of London, other children spoke of seeing

LEFT: The Fairies' Tree in Fitzroy Gardens, Melbourne, Australia.

ABOVE: A Cornish pixie charm.

OPPOSITE: Peter Vangslev-Nielsen, sexton of the Agerup folk church, near Holbaek, Denmark, holding a silver goblet reputed to have been part of a huge treasure stolen from the fairies.

a miniature biplane, piloted by a fairy. The plane, which had a wingspan of about a foot, swooped down into their garden, landing briefly, then took off again, the fairy pilot waving them a cheery goodbye.

According to a modern poll, a little over half the people of Iceland claim to believe in fairies, the difficulties and delays in building a new road near Akureyri, in 1984, having been attributed by the locals to fairy disapproval. Indeed, Iceland's Public Roads Administration has a policy of avoiding certain locations that, according to tradition, are inhabited by fairies, which Viktor Ingolfsson, a crime writer and employee of the

OPPOSITE: The Beara Peninsula, in the south-west of Ireland, where a fairy shoe was found in 1835.

BELOW: The Fairy Bridge at Dunvegan, Scotland, where the fairy wife of one of the MacLeod chieftains, the Lords of Skye, is said to have abandoned her husband and young son to return to fairyland.

was too narrow to be a doll's shoe, and was as exquisitely fashioned as any craftsman-made human shoe. The Beara shoe ended up at Harvard University, where scientists came to the conclusion that the material used was a mouse's skin.

Sir Arthur Conan Doyle, author of the Sherlock Holmes stories, and with a strong interest in the supernatural, had been commissioned by *Strand Magazine* to write an article on fairies for its Christmas 1920 issue. While

LEFT: & BELOW: Frances Griffiths with the fairies photographed by Elsie Wright in Cottingley, West Yorkshire, England, in 1917.

OPPOSITE: Elsie Wright in the 1980s, showing how she and Frances Griffiths were able to fake their fairy photographs by means of cutouts 60 years before. Both she and Frances continued to insist they had actually played with the fairies and were merely illustrating what they had seen.

company, cannily regards as hedging one's bets.

Fairy goblets are a recurring theme, and a silver cup, kept at the Agerup church near Holbaek, Denmark, is said to have been stolen from the fairies several hundred years ago. Tiny fairy-sized items of clothing have turned up in Ireland, including a coat, 6.5in (16.5cm) long, found in a fairy ring by Abraham Ffolliott in 1868. It was fully lined, with a velvet collar, and appeared to be well-worn, which could also be said of a tiny shoe found by a farm labourer on the Beara Peninsula, in the south-west of Ireland in 1835. Less than 2in (5cm) long, it

preparing this, news that actual photographs of fairies were in circulation came to his notice, which turned out to be the most convincing evidence of their existence so far: the photographs were of 16-year-old Elsie Wright and her younger cousin, Frances Griffiths, which they had taken themselves, and in which they are seen to be playing with fairies, which had become their friends, in a glen behind their house in Cottingley, Yorkshire. With such a high-profile figure as Conan Doyle on their side, who took the girls' pictures to be proof positive of the existence of fairies, and insisted on their publication in the magazine, the photographs soon came to be regarded as the most celebrated of their time, in which contemporary experts could find no evidence of trickery.

It was not until 1982 that Geoffrey Crawley, editor of the *British Journal of Photography*, made a more detailed examination, and found they had been faked by means of cut-out illustrations. Elsie and Frances, by now elderly women, immediately confessed this part of the deception, insisting that the pictures were simply a means of illustrating what they had seen with their own eyes.

CROWD PHENOMENA

Almost everyone has experienced what it is like to be part of a crowd, whether it be at a concert, demonstration or soccer match. It is a feeling that one's own emotions are being reinforced by the crowd as a whole, which usually leads to wholesale, spontaneous applause. But it can also lead to mass hallucinations, visions or illusions, or even wild panic attacks, and there are well-documented instances of all three.

When a single person claims to have seen something that cannot be explained by science, or thinks they have, then it's usually written off as neurosis or the product of an over-

RIGHT: A photograph of two faces, seen in the waves and taken from the SS Watertown *after they had been recognized by the crew as belonging to the two seamen who, a few days before, had been overcome by noxious fumes while cleaning out a cargo tank, had died, and were buried at sea. The camera was kept in safe keeping until the picture could be developed on reaching port at New Orleans.*

OPPOSITE: People in large crowds seem to relinquish their individuality, becoming part of Jung's 'collective unconscious'.

active imagination. When a group of people have the same vision, however, it is not so easily explained away, yet instances of this are known to have occurred throughout history. Visions at sea are a recurring theme, in which a virtually captive audience (the crew) claim to share the same traumatic experience. In his 1897 book, *Hallucinations and Illusions*, Edmund Parrish recalls the case of a ship's cook who, several days after he had died, was seen by the entire crew, walking across

the waves towards them with his characteristic limping gait. On nearing the ship, the vision dissolved into a piece of floating wreckage.

There is photographic evidence of a similar incident happening aboard the SS *Watertown* in December 1929, when two crewmen died and were buried at sea. Next day, and during the following two voyages, visions of the men were seen in the waves, always from the same point on the deck, with only their two ghostly heads poking above the water.

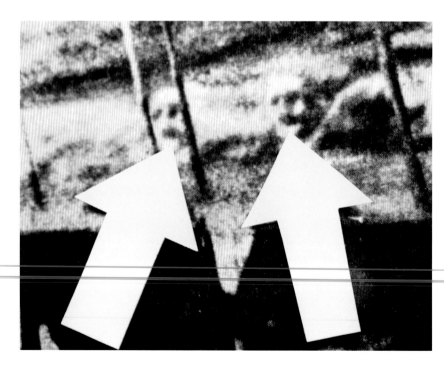

But there are are various explanations for mass visions, one being that an individual sees the vision first, then relates his experience to those who have experienced the same trauma (such as the death of a colleague), planting the suggestion firmly into their minds; the power of suggestion is based on the psychological mechanism that whatever the subconscious accepts it will act upon, even though the first person may have had no intention of setting such a process in motion. Another theory, according to the authors Bob Rickard and John Michell, holds that a medium or magician can often set off a mass vision intentionally, by creating 'a different order of reality' in which the crowd temporarily suspends its normal beliefs and faith in science.

OPPOSITE: Walking barefoot on hot coals in Sri Lanka.

RIGHT: A girl, paralyzed by a brain tumour, was on the verge of death when she was blessed during the great pilgrimge mass at Fatima on 13 August 1946. She was instantly cured.

BELOW: A statue group showing the Virgin Mary appearing to the three peasant children at Fatima.

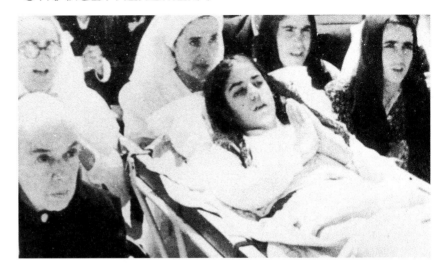

As long as people have faith in the power of the medium, then this is quite possible. In the case of fire-walking (see opposite) there is usually an overseer, who will either 'prepare' the fire-walkers, be they novices or more experienced, or else be the first to walk the hot coals himself. Faith, in its broadest sense, seems to be the key to success in events such as these.

Religious faith can produce similar effects, and there are cases of entire congregations sharing a vision along with their priest. It may not be necessary for the priest to suggest to the crowd what it might see, yet all involved will claim afterwards to have seen the same thing. In the famous case

of the three peasant children at Fatima, Portugal, in 1917, Lucia dos Santos and her cousins, Jacinta and Francisco Marto, claimed to have seen a recurring vision of the Virgin Mary. No one else was able to see the vision, but the children said it had promised a miracle on 13 October. On that day, 50,000 people turned up, and all claimed to have seen the sun 'dance' or tremble and move around in the sky before moving towards the crowd. Did all these people share the same hallucination, or was a true miracle taking place?

One vision that certainly does not deserve to be classed as such is the Indian rope trick. This, in its classic form, consists of a magician's boy helper shinning up a rope, which the watching crowd perceives to be standing in mid-air, with no visible means of support. Then the magician follows with a knife, and both vanish somewhere at the top of the rope. There are screams, and dismembered parts of the boy's body fall to the ground, followed by the magician

LEFT: The Indian rope trick.

OPPOSITE: Carnac, in Brittany, France.

himself holding his gory knife. He collects the body parts into a box, says the magic word, and the boy reappears whole and unharmed.

It all seems very real as far as the crowd is concerned, but films of the rope trick show magician and boy to be simply standing by a coil of rope lying on the ground. The upright rope, the boy and the magician climbing it, and the whole grisly scene that follows, are in fact a mass illusion, skilfully induced by performers who know how to work a crowd.

Exactly the same effect can be achieved even when a crowd is not occupying the same physical space. In an astonishing demonstration of the power of the modern media, Orson Welles was able to convince a good section of America's population that aliens were invading planet Earth. This occurred in October 1938, when Welles' version of H.G. Wells's novel, *The War of the Worlds*, was broadcast to the nation from the studios of CBS.

Instead of being a straight radio dramatization of the novel it was presented in the form of intensely realistic news bulletins, presumably being broadcast in real time, which described alien machines advancing

upon New York. The mass panic that ensued was to a large extent magnified by the newspapers, but many inhabitants of New York and New Jersey continued to believe an invasion had taken place. Police, hospitals, newspapers and bus stations were all contacted by citizens desperate to know what they should do, while distant family and friends were frantically warned. Could this happen in the 21st

century? These days we are far more accustomed to bombardment by news of genuine disasters, while new opportunities have been presented by the internet for spreading spurious rumours at lightning speed.

LEY LINES

The people who built the great megalithic structures of north-western Europe – Stonehenge, Avebury, Carnac

in Brittany and so on – were far more advanced than is often believed. Not only did these constructions involve a deep understanding of mathematics and astronomy, but also formidable powers of organization and a massive commitment of resources. Silbury Hill, for example, only a couple of miles from the huge stone circle at Avebury in Wiltshire, England, is a large, cone-shaped mound, 130ft (40m) high and covering 5 acres (2.2 hectares). It took an estimated 18 million man-hours to build which, according to archeologist Richard Atkinson, was the equivalent of the economic commitment to the space programme of the United States. These structures on their own were in every sense great achievements.

But it is possible they were only a part of a much wider scheme, which would have needed extensive planning, surveying and geographical knowledge to construct. The location of the sites, rather than having been chosen at random or for a particular purpose,

LEFT: Stonehenge, Wiltshire, England.

OPPOSITE: Silbury Hill, also in Wiltshire, is a prehistoric mound believed to be some 4,500 years old.

were actually built to be in geometric alignment with one another, but it was not until 1909 that Sir Norman Lockyer, the British Astronomer-Royal, offered some evidence that this might actually be the case.

He noticed that the line of the midsummer sunrise, if traced 6 miles (10km) south-west from Stonehenge, arrived at the Neolithic settlement and religious centre of Grovely Castle, while Old Sarum, another important hilltop settlement, was also exactly 6 miles from Stonehenge, the three sites forming a near-perfect equilateral triangle. The later Salisbury Cathedral, moreover, on which work began in AD 1220, was found to be on the same line as Old Sarum and Stonehenge.

It was a controversial theory, which in the absence of written records from the time was impossible to prove. Lockyer's contemporaries were dismissive, arguing that only primitive tribes, totally devoid of the skills necessary to construct anything so complex, would have existed at that time. They also argued that Britain, in particular, possessed so many ancient sites that it would be an easy task to find some which followed a straight line, and that any deliberate attempt to

Glastonbury Tor, reputed to be the focus of King Arthur's Avalon.

form an alignment was unlikely and would have been merely a coincidence.

This did nothing to deter Alfred Watkins, a Herefordshire businessman and antiquarian, who in the 1920s took Lockyer's theory a step further, claiming that Britain was crisscrossed with a network of what he called ley lines, that linked ancient and sacred sites in a deliberate way. Lockyer's triangle, he decided, could be extended, with Stonehenge, Avebury and Glastonbury forming a right-angled triangle. The line linking Avebury and Glastonbury would be in line with the May Day sunrise, and extending this line south-west would cross Cadbury Castle in Somerset, Brent Tor in Devon, and St. Michael's Mount in Cornwall in what was the longest possible stretch of unbroken land in southern Britain.

Similarly, the line of the midsummer sunrise that ran through Stonehenge could be extended north-east to Inkpen Beacon and the Neolithic Winterborne Camp, while heading the other way, beyond Grovely Castle, it would slice across the Cerne

OPPOSITE: Avebury's standing stones.

RIGHT: The Cerne Abbas Giant.

Abbas Giant (a huge chalk figure on a Dorset hillside), hitting the coast at Puncknowle Beacon on the south coast. Both lines were over 200 miles (320km) long, and linked ancient sites, churches, castles and tors.

Watkins published a book in 1925, *The Old Straight Track*, which also included the less probable theory that ley lines were old trade routes. While it is true that pre-Roman trackways tended to keep to high ground, for the purely practical reason that it made them more passable throughout the year, and that a dead straight alignment would have led the traveller up hill, down dale and through many a boggy valley. Once the Roman Empire had spread itself across Europe, the roads built by the Romans used a different approach, utilizing high points as waymarkers with straight lines in between, the superior construction, surfacing and drainage making them usable all-year-round, whatever the terrain over which they passed.

Watkins's ley lines were greeted by many archeologists with the same

31

OPPOSITE: Salisbury Cathedral.

LEFT: Brent Tor, Devon, England, which may originally have been the site of an Iron Age hill fort.

derision to which Lockyer had been subjected, and opinion is divided to this day: some regard ley lines as 'New Age' nonsense, while Watkins's supporters claim to have found many more ley lines criss-crossing Britain. A common criticism is that the Watkins lines link sites that are centuries younger than the supposed Neolithic alignments and, as Lockyer's critics made clear, there are countless such sites across Britain, making it possible to link not a few of them along a straight line.

Many of the sites, however, are unlikely to be there by pure chance, having strong religious or mythological significance in common. And while it is true that many of Watkins's link points are of different ages, it is also true that later religious centres were built upon the sites of earlier ones, the earliest Christian missionaries having arrived with instructions not to destroy pagan sites but to build new churches on top of them. So the presence of churches hundreds of years younger than the

LEFT: St. Michael's Mount, Cornwall.

BELOW RIGHT: The Mowing Devil, an engraving dating from 1678 and possibly an early report of a crop circle.

Neolithic may signify the presence of much older foundations along the leys. Interestingly, many of the later churches dotted along the May Day sunrise line are dedicated to the dragon-killing saints, Michael and George. Can this be a coincidence, or is it evidence of something far more significant?

CROP CIRCLES

Since the phenomenon reasserted itself in the 1970s, crop circles have become the subject of various paranormal and fringe beliefs, one being that they are messages from extraterrestrials. Because many of them have tended to appear near ancient sites, such as at Stonehenge and in the vicinity of barrows and chalk horses in England, they have come to be included in New Age belief systems, some maintaining they are related to ley lines, and produce detectable energy when dowsed. Members of New Age religions sometimes gather at crop circles to meditate or because they believe they can use them as a means of contacting spirits.

The more pragmatic among us, however, say that they are created by freak meteorological conditions, such as when localized columns of ionized air (plasma vortices/vortexes) form over standing crops, while others attribute their formation to atmospheric phenomena such as freak tornadoes or ball lightning.

The crop circles that made their appearance between 1970 and 2000 usually took the form of simple circular patterns of various sizes, but more elaborate and complex geometrical

patterns gradually began to emerge. In general, the earlier formations appear to have been based on the principles of sacred geometry, but after 2000 appear to be more mathematical in form, having been based on fractal geometry, in which similar patterns recur at progressively smaller scales, while elements of three-dimensionality have also become more frequent,

ABOVE: A crop circle from 1996 on Stonehenge Down.

OPPOSITE: Crop circles from 2001 near the ancient site of Silbury Hill.

culminating in spectacular cuboid designs. Today, the design of crop circles has evolved to such an extent that they have come to be regarded as art forms in themselves.

The belief that they are of supernatural origin still persists, however, despite evidence to the contrary. Some say they have seen UFOs and other lights in the sky hovering in the vicinity of crop circles, while others claim to have photographed UFOs overflying them and creating the crop circles themselves, even though the images have usually been indistinct or clearly manufactured. The main criticism of crop circles having been created spontaneously by non-human forces is scant, and it is more believable to suppose they are the work of human pranksters. Indeed there have been cases where researchers have pronounced a crop circle 'genuine', only to be confronted at a later date by the people who fraudulently created them (usually a nocturnal activity), some of whom actually demonstrating how the deed had been done.

In 1976, Doug Bower and Dave Chorley, from Southampton, England, inspired by the Tully Saucer Nest,

which occurred in Queensland, Australia on 19 January 1966, decided to make their own crop circles as a joke. Using a 4ft (1.2m) long plank attached to a rope, it was a simple matter to create circles of 8ft in diameter, and they were able to make a 40-ft (12-m) circle in 15 minutes. Disappointed by the paucity of significant publicity following their efforts, they decided to go one step further, and in 1981 created a circle in the Matterley Bowl, a natural amphitheatre located just outside Winchester, Hampshire. But when others attributed their work to natural phenomena, Bower and Chorley made their designs increasingly complicated. Eventually, fearing his wife suspected him of adultery, due to his many nocturnal absences, Bower confessed and subsequently they both owned up to a British national newspaper.

This remarkable, strangely beautiful crop circle, discovered on 9 June 2001 at Berwick Bassett, near Avebury, is the type of organized harmonic form that has been adopted elsewhere. It is based upon rotating convex triangles containing the standing crop, which at the same time create other triangles within the laid crop.

FABULOUS BEASTS

Sea Monsters

Apemen

Spectral Hounds

Homing Animals

Big Cats Abroad

Werewolves

CHAPTER TWO
FABULOUS BEASTS

SEA MONSTERS

'I was shocked to full wakefulness by a swishing noise to starboard. I looked out over the water and suddenly saw the writhing, twisting shape of a great creature. It was outlined by the phosphorescence in the sea as if a string of neon lights were hanging from it. It was an enormous size, some 35 or more feet long, and it came towards me quite fast…It headed straight at me and disappeared beneath me…I stopped rowing. I was frozen with terror at this apparition. I forced myself to turn my head to look over the port

RIGHT: An image of a sea monk, a monster that appears in the 1864 edition of The Book of Days. *It has been described in travellers' tales since the time when it was believed that the sea held the equivalent of every creature that could be found on land.*

OPPOSITE: Giant octopuses and squid may have fuelled the rumours of sea monsters.

side. I saw nothing, but after a brief pause I heard a tremendous splash…Chay and I had seen whales and sharks, dolphins and porpoises, flying fish – all sorts of sea creatures – but this monster in the night was none of these. I reluctantly had to believe that there was only one thing it could have been – a sea serpent.'

So wrote Captain John Ridgway, who rowed across the Atlantic in 1966 in company with Chay Blythe, the quotation coming from their straightforward account of the trip, *A Fighting Chance.* But sailors have been sighting giants of the deep for generations before Ridgway and Blythe, be they massive squid, octopuses or sea serpents. It is certainly a beguiling thought that even today, especially where they are ultra-deep, the oceans have scarcely been explored by man, making the possibility of giant sea monsters certainly seem more feasible than the presence of unknown, unseen creatures on land.

How much more likely was the prospect of sea monsters a few centuries ago, when the sea was even more dangerous and unknown than it is today. The French naturalist, Pierre Denys de Montfort, made a collection of mariners' accounts in the 18th century, that included one of a giant octopus attacking a man in a ship's rigging. Fighting it off, the sailors

chopped off one of its tentacles, which measured 23ft (7m). In 1861 the French corvette *Alecton* battled for several hours with a giant squid. It was killed, the seamen intending to bring the carcase home as proof of its existence, but it rotted badly and had to be tossed back overboard. The existence of these creatures was to be proved in the years that followed, when carcases washed up on the east coasts of America and Canada were identified as such, their tentacles measuring in the region of a staggering 43ft (13m) long.

But squid are not sea monsters, whose existence has not been helped by certain well-publicized hoaxes. The American archeologist, Dr. Albert C. Koch, claimed to have unearthed the skeleton of a sea serpent in Alabama in the 1840s. It was 115ft (35m) long, but turned out to be a collection of bones from different animals, which Koch had pieced together. Koch actually made

OPPOSITE: The vast expanses of the oceans still conceal many mysteries.

RIGHT: Dr. Dewitt Webb, photographed on 30 November 1896 at Anastasia Beach, Florida, with a washed-up carcase that was subsequently identified as a giant octopus.

genuine discoveries, too, even though his sea serpent had proved to be a fake.

The same was true of one of the most famous photographs of all time, claimed to be that of a sea monster. For nearly 60 years the picture of 'Nessie', otherwise the Loch Ness monster, and taken by London surgeon, R. Kenneth Wilson, was accepted as authentic. He

snapped the creature in April 1934, only a year after a 'sighting' of it had stimulated interest in the subject around the world, prompting many to come forward to confirm that they, too, had seen the beast.

Wilson's picture certainly seemed genuine enough, with Nessie's long neck poking up out of the loch's waters in

LEFT: On 25 April 1977, the Japanese trawler Zuiyo Maru *found this strange carcase in its nets 30 miles (50km) off Christchurch, New Zealand. It was widely thought to be a plesiosaur and caused something of a sensation back in Japan, while others were more sceptical and suggested it might be the decomposed remains of a basking shark.*

BELOW: Morgawr, the Cornish sea monster, was photographed in 1976 from Rosemullion Head, near Falmouth, Cornwall.

OPPOSITE: A model of 'Nessie', based on photographic sightings.

classic style. But it was exposed as a fraud in 1993, when Christian Spurling made a confession to the effect on his deathbed. He had been encouraged, he said, by his stepfather, and Wilson's 'monster' had been no more than a head and neck made up of plastic and wood, about a foot tall, mounted on a toy submarine. Spurling's step-father, having been a party in the deception, had left Nessie's 'footprints' on the shoreline, that had been achieved by means of an ashtray set into a hippopotomus's foot.

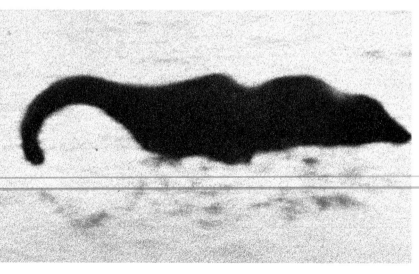

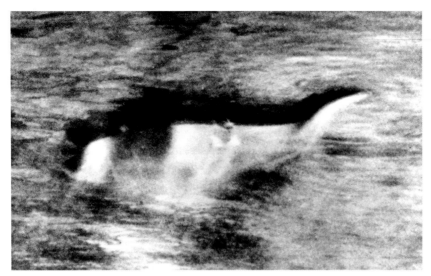

LEFT & BELOW LEFT: Could this be more evidence that the Loch Ness Monster exists?

OPPOSITE: Photogenic Urquhart Castle stands beside Loch Ness in Scotland.

But Nessie has had many serious researchers, notably Tim Dinsdale, whose film of what appears to be the monster swimming was analyzed by the RAF and accepted as genuine evidence, while Robert Rhine, from the Academy of Applied Sciences in Chicago, took an underwater picture of what appeared to be a large, long-necked creature in 1975.

But it has to be admitted that no cast-iron evidence has ever been presented supporting the existence of sea serpents, sea monsters or whatever one likes to call them, either in Loch Ness or in the wider oceans. Giant squid and octopuses there may be, but the jury is still out where the more fabulous beasts are concerned.

APEMEN

From the yeti of the Himalayas to North America's Bigfoot, and innumerable apes in between, there seems to be a perennial fascination with the idea of a forgotten species, perhaps

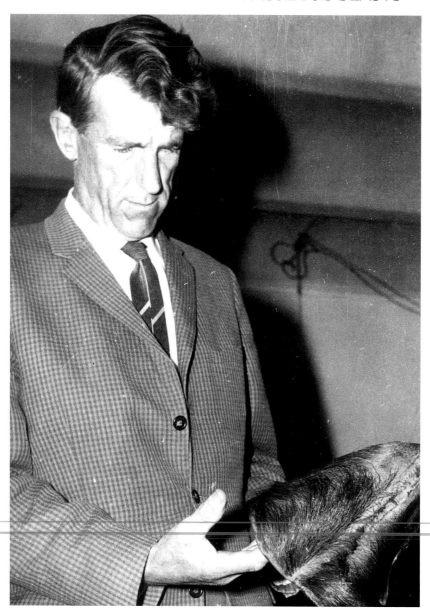

the elusive 'missing link', that some believe still roams the wilder parts of the planet, waiting to be discovered. There have been claimed sightings and stories of hairy, dwarf-like creatures, aquatic apes, and muscle-bound two-legged monsters up to 16ft (5m) tall. Bernard Heuvelmans in *On the Track of the Unknown Animals,* describes it as '... a huge creature, half-man, half-beast; it lives in caves high and inaccessible in the mountains. The skin of its face is white; the body is covered with a thick coat of dark hair. Its arms, like those of anthropoid apes, reach down to its knees, but its face looks rather more human. Its thick legs are bowed; its toes turn inward – some say they even turn backward. It is very muscular and can uproot trees and lift up boulders of remarkable size.'

OPPOSITE LEFT: Sir Edmund Hillary is pictured here in Calcutta, India, holding the hairy scalp which, according to Himalayan villagers, is that of a yeti.

OPPOSITE RIGHT: A yeti's footprint, photographed in 1951 in the Menlung Basin of the Himalayas.

RIGHT: A mountain in Nepal, where yetis have been heard calling to one another.

This is not a modern phenomenon. In 1811 explorer David Thompson discovered 14-in (36-cm) tracks near Jasper, Alberta, which he put down to a Sasquatch, the Native American name for a Bigfoot. Just as stories abound of alien abductions so also are there accounts of people claiming to have been carried off by apemen and who have survived to tell the tale. An early example was the experience of lumberman, Albert Ostman, who in 1924 was camping opposite Vancouver Island. Asleep in his sleeping bag, he later told how he was picked up by a Bigfoot and carried 25 miles (40km) back to its lair, where a female and two young also lived. Ostman claimed to have been well treated by the Bigfoot family, giving the reason why he had

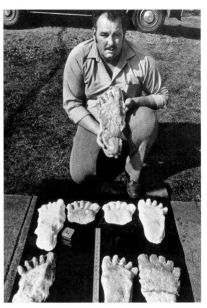

ABOVE: *Paul Freeman, a cryptozoologist, claimed to have seen a Bigfoot in Umatilla National Forest, Oregon, on 10 June 1982 and also on other occasions. He made casts of their footprints which showed dermal ridges.*

LEFT: *A photograph of what appears to be a dead Sasquatch, found in 1911 in a trapper's cabin at Lillooet, British Columbia.*

Frame 352 from a motion film purporting to be that of a Bigfoot female, made by Roger Patterson and Robert Gimlin on 20 October 1967 at Bluff Creek, Northern California.

kept silent for over 30 years as a fear of ridicule.

Even more extraordinary is the story that appeared in the *National Bulletin* on 30 June 1969, with the headline, 'I was raped by the Abominable Snowman'. An American girl claimed to have been caught by the creature in woods in Minnesota and almost raped (an example of the usual sub-editor's poetic licence) before she managed to shoot it in the eye and escape. This was supposedly the same hominid that had been used as a touring exhibit by showman Frank D. Hansen. Hansen claimed to have shot the creature, or to have found it floating in a block of ice in Siberia, or to have substituted the original with a model – his story varied over time. But he was convincing enough to persuade two reputable zoologists, Ivan Sanderson and Bernard Heuvelmans, to give it some cautious scientific approval. But John Napier, of Birkbeck College, University of London, was more

with a whole community of Bigfoot hunters, researchers and authors carry on with their quest into the 21st century. In August 1998, Wes Sumerlin claimed to have found fresh Bigfoot tracks in the Blue Mountains of Washington State. He claimed that he and his family had had many encounters with the creatures over the previous 50 years, and that he had become so familiar with particular individuals that he had given them names. He claimed to have once got to within 50ft (15m) of Buckskin, a female he had seen before: 'When she turned to look my way, she was real visible and so were her breasts, so I knew it was a female,' adding that the creatures he saw were something more than mere animals: 'No, I think he's far more intelligent than other animals. He has a face something like a human, but it isn't exactly a human face either.'

Bigfoot's natural habitat may be the mountains and woods of North America, but the yeti's is the snow-covered slopes of the Himalayan mountains. Again, there have been plenty of supposed sightings and footprints photographed, but no one has ever been able to present more concrete evidence, such as a body. As

with Bigfoot, much of the evidence can be explained, such as footprints having become enlarged as the snow around them melts. The langur monkey has been seen in the Himalayas at heights of over 13,125ft (4000m), and stands on two legs; one 1944 expedition gave a description that matched that of the monkey, though it was thought to have been the same size as a man. In 1970, the respected mountaineer, Don Whillans, saw an 'ape-like creature', again probably a langur, bounding along a ridge in the moonlight.

Do any of these apemen actually exist? Given the efforts to find Bigfoot over the years, without a single piece of hard evidence having been unearthed but a good few hoaxes uncovered along the way, one must conclude that it seems rather unlikely.

LEFT: A Bigfoot, photographed on 11 July 1995 by a forest patrol officer at Wild Creek in the foothills of Mount Rainier in Washington state.

OPPOSITE: The Myakka Skunk-Ape (Floridian Bigfoot), claimed to have been photographed in 2000 in Sarasota County, Florida, as it was helping itself to apples from an elderly couple's porch.

difficult to deceive, and after examining the exhibit reported that it was made of latex rubber and expanded polystyrene. It had been superbly crafted but was still a model for all that.

Footprints, sightings, accounts, and even film of the supposed lost ape of North America, continue to appear,

SPECTRAL HOUNDS

The animal most commonly seen in phantom form is a black dog, sometimes referred to as a hell-hound, a dog of doom, or a Church Grim. Such a creature is central to the famous Sherlock Holmes novel, *The Hound of the Baskervilles*, that was possibly based on the Black Shuck of East Anglia, even though the action of the story takes place among the quagmires and swirling mists of Dartmoor, Devon, in England's West Country.

Tales of these spectral hounds have been told for hundreds of years and can be heard the length and breadth of Britain. One of the most recent, perhaps, is the one connected with the death of the British composer, Lionel Monckton, who died in 1924.

One day, some of Monckton's friends, including Donald Calthrop, were sitting chatting at their club when Calthrop had a sudden premonition that all was not right as far as Monckton was concerned. He suddenly became aware of a black dog, standing in the corner of the room. His companions did not share the experience, however, and dismissed

LEFT: The appearance of the Black Dog of Bungay, Suffolk, in England, made such an impression on the locals that its image appears on items throughout the town.

OPPOSITE: The magnificent church of the Holy Trinity at Blythburgh, Suffolk. Black Shuck attempted to enter the church, leaving scorchmarks behind where he had scratched at the door.

it as mere imagination. A few hours later, the tragic news arrived that Monckton had died – apparently at the precise moment that Calthrop had seen the black dog.

But there was an even more terrifying manifestation on 4 August 1577, in Bungay, Suffolk. Most of the townsfolk were gathered together in St. Mary's Church, when a violent thunderstorm was unexpectedly unleashed. Suddenly a black dog appeared, illuminated by the intermittant bursts of lightning.

Everyone saw the creature as it ran down the aisle, and two people died of fright where they knelt in prayer. A third was also affected, and although they survived, were left shrivelled and bent. The church tower collapsed in through the roof and the church's

north door was left bearing scorchmarks, that can still be seen to this day.

What they had seen was the fearful creature known as the Black Shuck. Described as a devil-dog, it has been seen wandering the East Anglian countryside since Viking times, being a large dog, sometimes as big as a horse, with malevolent flaming eyes that glow red or green.

The Black Shuck also seems to have had connections with Hugh Bigod, the Earl of Norfolk, who staged a rebellion against Henry II in 1173. Legend has it that to guarantee his success Bigod made a pact with the Devil, forfeiting his soul. The Devil tricked him, however, and his army was defeated, forcing him to surrender his property that included Bungay Castle. He challenged the Devil, however, who by way of compromise transformed him into a black devil-dog.

Blythburgh church in Suffolk, a magnificent building known as the Cathedral of the Marshes, also bears the scorchmarks of Black Shuck's claws on its door, when, as at Bungay, he tried to enter it. This time, it seems, the power of

The scorchmarks left by Black Shuck are still visible on Blythburgh church's door.

prayer was able to save the church's parishioners.

HOMING ANIMALS

Migrations of animals and birds are among the wonders of the natural world. Every year, four million greater shearwaters make the journey from northern Europe to Tristan da Cunha, the group of tiny islands in the South Atlantic. Arctic terns make the trip from North America, Siberia and Europe to the Antarctic and back again, a 25,000-mile (40230-km) journey that entails flying for 24 hours a day for eight months of the year.

These flights are not only incredible feats of endurance but they also pose the question as to how birds are able to navigate such huge distances with such accuracy. Blue whales and Arctic whales travel thousands of miles across oceans, bats cover huge distances, returning to one particular cave where they always roost, while salmon will cross oceans to find the particular river estuary where they habitually spawn.

A wild salmon, making its epic journey upstream from the sea in order to spawn.

FABULOUS BEASTS

LEFT: Arctic terns make incredible flights from North America, Siberia and Northern Europe to the Antarctic, with the result that they are continuously on the wing for eight months of the year.

OPPOSITE: Bats cover huge distances too, returning to the same cave to roost.

The sun, the stars, magnetic forces, the ability of some creatures to see polarized light or detect minute changes in water temperature, are all possible means of navigation, the simple truth being that no one knows for sure how this is accomplished. It may be that some sort of homing instinct or race memory is passed down the generations, exerting an irresistible compulsion to head for the same place.

But this does little to explain the many accounts of domesticated pets, which find their way home even when their owners have in the interim moved house. Such stories are relatively common, appearing in newspapers across the world, and some of them are possibly cases of mistaken identity; of course, most owners would love to believe their missing pet has gone through hell and high water to find them. This does not explain the many

genuine cases of dogs and cats (and the odd hedgehog and rabbit, together with the inevitable pigeon) which have been able to find their own way home. Indeed, it is such a common occurrence that Disney even made a film based on the phenomenon, *The Incredible Journey*, which doesn't make it any the less strange.

Some of the distances involved are indeed incredible, especially where animals have hitched lifts on some form of transport or other. A collie dog (the name is not recorded) was sent to Calcutta by its owner, who lived near the port of Inverkeithing in Scotland. Once in India, the dog disappeared, but a few months later turned up at the house of its old master, showing its delight at being home again. In the absence of someone having put the dog onto the right boat, it must have stowed

itself away on a Dundee-bound ship at Calcutta docks (one suggestion is that it recognized the Scottish accents!), then happened to find a smaller vessel heading up the coast to its home town.

Another such homing story concerns a terrier named Hector, a ship's dog belonging to a first officer on the Dutch ship *Simaloer*. In April 1922 it was accidentally left behind in Vancouver while the ship sailed on to Japan. There were five other ships waiting at the quay, and Hector managed to pick the one bound for Yokohama. Eighteen days later, as the ship docked, the dog began to bark excitedly at a small boat by the wharf. It was *Simaloer*'s tender, and one of the two men on board was his owner. Similar to this is the tale of Puss, a white Persian cat, which trekked 1,000 miles (1600km) across Australia in 1977. The journey took 12 months, but Puss was able to find the right state, the right street and the right house.

In some ways it is easier to understand how animals find their way home, but harder when their owners have moved away. Sugar, an American cat, walked 1,500 miles (2415km) from Gage, Oklahoma, where it had been rehoused with neighbours, to

Anderson, California, where its original family now had its new home. The family recognized the cat from the slight deformity of its left hip joint, and the whole story was thoroughly investigated by the ESP researcher, Dr. J.B. Rhine.

Studies on animal homing instincts suggest that feats like this are not unique: Dr. Bastian Schmid describes an experiment in which a number of dogs were taken from their homes in a closed van and driven by a circuitous route to a place miles away. In every case the dog seemed temporarily confused when released, but was soon able to get its bearings and head off in the right direction. Experiments with cats show similar results.

But what such experiments fail to tell us is how they are able do this; what is not in doubt is that they have powers of navigation which we still do not fully understand.

BIG CATS ABROAD

In many parts of the world, big cats – lions, pumas, panthers, leopards – are a fact of life, but in Britain they have been extinct in the wild for thousands of years, and in such a small and densely populated island most would

accept that this is indeed the case. Yet claimed sightings and scare stories of big cats still roaming Britain persist. Time and again there has been circumstantial evidence of footprints, clawmarks and the killing or mutilation of sheep, cattle, deer and horses, in a way that suggests that a large and powerful feline was responsible. But like the Loch Ness Monster or Bigfoot, no one has yet produced incontrovertible proof, in the form of a

ABOVE: Are large cats like this roaming wild where they are not supposed to be?

OPPOSITE LEFT: This freshly-killed sheep in North Devon, its throat ripped out, appears to have fallen victim to an unusual predator.

OPPOSITE RIGHT: This cast of a footprint measures 4in (10cm) across, and may well belong to a big cat on the loose in the English countryside.

clear photograph or a dead body, that this was the case, neither has a big cat ever turned up as a roadkill, which is a common enough sight in Britain.

It could be that some of these sightings are of pets which may have escaped or been set free. Farmer Ted Noble trapped a puma near Loch Ness in 1980, but felt that 'Felicity' was too tame and too well-fed to have lived a life in the wild. The Dangerous Wild Animals Act of 1976 obliges owners of such big cats to licence them, which is not cheap, and it could be that some are selfish enough to set their animals free rather than pay up.

But that still doesn't explain the level of sightings and livestock killings that have occurred before and since the act. The 'Surrey Puma' was big news in 1962, and no less than 362 reported sightings were made to the Godalming police over a period of two years, encouraging even more amateur hunters to set forth; none of them even saw it. The same is true of the 'Shooters Hill' cheetah of 1963, the police taking a more active role this time after a large, golden creature leaped over the hood of one of their patrol cars. One hundred and twenty-six policemen went out looking for the

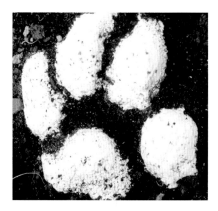

beast, accompanied by dogs, the army and animal welfare officials but found nothing. Major hunts were also organized to pursue the Beasts of Bodmin and Exmoor, after a outbreak of sheep killings had been reported in these rural areas.

But evidence of big cat activity is not only restricted to the rural parts of Britain. In the London suburb of Sydenham in spring 2005, a man reported having been attacked by a black panther early one morning while putting his cat out. The clawmarks on his arm seemed real enough, and at around the same time farmers in Oxfordshire, plagued by cattle killings, were offering a reward of £5,000 for the capture of a 'large, black animal'.

Big cats may or may not still be roaming where they should not be, but

OPPOSITE: While the cougar (puma or mountain lion) is indigenous to the Americas it is not a native of Britain, but animals resembling it have nevertheless been spotted there.

LEFT: Tracks left in the snow indicate the typical bounding gait of a cat, and the fact that the pad marks are set 54in (137cm) apart suggests it was a big one.

there is little doubt that winged cats are something of a reality. They may seem to be ideal companions for witches on their broomsticks, but there really have been cases of cats with furry growths on their backs resembling wings. They might not be able to fly like a bird, but they are certainly able to make impressive leaps.

One day in 1933, Mrs Hughes-Griffiths of Oxford, England, saw an odd-looking cat in her garden. It then proceeded to leap from the ground up onto a high beam in her stable block, 'using its wings in a similar manner as a bird'. It was captured by men from the Oxford Zoo, and one of them, W.E. Sawyer, confirmed later to having '... examined the cat tonight, and there is no doubt about the wings. They grow just in front of the hindquarters.' A few

OPPOSITE: Regarded as a brave and intelligent animal in ancient times, the wolf has come to be a creature to be feared, being an amalgam of the werewolf and the Big Bad Wolf.

LEFT: A winged cat, photographed in 1899. There are three possible explanations: the wings are large matted wadges of hair, caused by a lack of grooming; they are the result of a skin condition known as feline cutaneous asthenia or FCA; they are an abnormality in the form of conjoining or extra limbs.

BELOW: A young cat, which developed wings measuring 11in (28cm) as it grew. It also had a broad, flat tail.

years later, another British winged cat, Sally, came to public notice because of her 2-ft (0.6-m) wingspan that allowed her to make giant leaps. Both of these cats appear to have been well cared for, but this has not always been the case. In 1966, three such cats were reported in Ontario, Canada, all of which had been shot, the third by Jean Revers as it attempted to attack a local cat from the air, 'making gliding jumps of fifty or sixty feet – wings extended'.

WEREWOLVES
Werewolves, also known as lycanthropes, have long featured in folklore as persons with the ability to shape-shift into wolf-like creatures, either by magic or after being placed

FABULOUS BEASTS

Strangely enough, there have also been were-tigers, not to mention were-hyenas, cats, hares, foxes, bears and even weasels. But werewolves feature in the most common and enduring of the shape-shifting stories. Every country in Europe has its own such myths and legends, which vary in detail from place to place.

Werewolves have occasionally been regarded as benign creatures, cast in the role of protecting their human benefactors. They are not always male, although 'were' in Old English derives

LEFT: An old woodcut of a werewolf.

BELOW: A scene from the film An American Werewolf in London, *starring David Naughton.*

OPPOSITE: The High Caucasus of Armenia, where tales of werewolves have long proliferated.

from the word for 'man'. In Armenian folklore, women often became werewolves as a punishment for their sins, after being visited by spirits which

under a curse, a transformation often linked with the appearance of the full moon. There is evidence, however, that the phenomenon was also known to the Ancient Greeks and Romans, and there can be few legends that have become so widespread or that have persisted for so long. The story was eventually translated into the horror films of the 1950s and '60s, although by the 1980s, the success of the comedy film, *An American Werewolf in London*, suggests that the public's terror of the half-man, half-wolf was starting to wear a little thin.

ordered them to wear wolfskins which would create in them a craving for human flesh. They would then devour their children, prowling at night and killing and eating other children once their own were gone. By reversing the process, i.e. shedding their wolfskins at dawn, they were then able to revert to their human form.

In 16th-century Europe, supposed werewolves were caught and burned in large numbers, especially in France, there being parallels here with the persecution of witches, whereby the troubles of a community could be blamed on a single individual. Burning at the stake was originally thought to

be sufficient to kill werewolves, although a silver bullet was later seen as an infallible means of finishing them off for good. They were also thought to be vulnerable to the plant wolfsbane, to three blows on the forehead with a knife, or to the drawing of three drops of blood.

Evidence for the existence of these creatures, as opposed to the innumerable legends about them, has been presented in the bizarre way some victims have met their deaths. A story appeared in *Cornhill Magazine* in October 1918 of a Captain Shott, who had been working in northern Nigeria. His village had recently been raided by

hyenas, but hunters were surprised to find that their tracks turned into human footprints at a certain point. Captain Shott's group caught up with one of the animals one night, and shot off its jaw. It ran off, but they followed the bloody trail to another village, where another man died the next day, his jaw having also been shot off.

A more recent example is quoted in *Occult in the Orient*, a book by C. Dane. In 1960 Harold Young, an official in Thailand, was hunting in the mountains when he heard that a *taw*, a jungle werewolf, was in the vicinity. Hearing screams coming from a village hut, he rushed in to see a *taw* savaging a woman. He shot it in the flank but it escaped, and next day a man was found with a similar bullet wound in his side. Did Shott and Young really experience this phenomena, or were they the result of over-active imagination?

There are certainly plenty of medical theories to explain the concept,

ABOVE LEFT: A werewolf attacking a man, a woodcut from Johann Geller von Kaiserberg's Die Emeis, *1516.*

OPPOSITE: Thailand, where jungle werewolves are known as taws.

one being that the stories arose to account for the deeds of human serial killers, whose indulgence in cannibalism, mutilation and cyclical killings could be cited as 'proof' that a werewolf was responsible. Conditions such as porphyria and hypertrichosis can cause excessive hair growth in human beings,

while another variation on the theme is a high sensitivity to light, causing its sufferers to venture abroad only at night.

The word lycanthropy is also used to describe a mental condition, thankfully very rare, in which sufferers genuinely believe they can transform themselves into animals. In northern

Spain in the 1850s, Manuel Blanco Romasanto was tried for the murder of several women. He confessed he was a werewolf, saying to the judge: 'Were I to become a wolf, even you, a rational man, would be so terrified that you could not fire the gun, and even if you did, the bullets could never harm me.'

AWESOME EDIFICES

The Great Pyramid at Giza

The Nazca Lines

Megalithic Engineering

Stonehenge

The Great Wall of China

CHAPTER THREE

AWESOME EDIFICES

THE GREAT PYRAMID AT GIZA

Egypt's pyramids continue to attract more admiration and controversy than any other man-made structures in history. Of the 200 or more existing in Egypt, it is the three pyramids of the Giza Necropolis, located a dozen or so miles from Cairo, which generate the most interest, being all that remain of the Seven Wonders of the Ancient World. But how were they built and what was their purpose? It would be more than a challenge for modern civil engineers to build structures of this size today, but to have constructed them 7,000 years ago, with only primitive tools, seems little short of a miracle.

Perhaps this is why so much conjecture has become attached to

RIGHT: The Great Sphinx, said to bear the likeness of Khafre, seen against the backdrop of Khufu's Great Pyramid.

OPPOSITE: The three pyramids of the Giza Necropolis.

them: that they were built by a super-race of extraterrestrial beings; that the weight of the Great Pyramid equals the weight of the Earth divided by one thousand billion; or that the limestone blocks were not quarried as solid stones at all, but moulded from a type of limestone cement. Sir Flinders Petrie, the respected archeologist, would have described some of the more outlandish of these theories as 'pyramidiocy'.

What is undeniable is the sheer scale of Khufu's Great Pyramid and the accuracy of its construction. Two-and-a-half million blocks of limestone were used, and surveyors in Napoleonic times calculated that, with the two adjacent pyramids of Khafre and Menkaure, there was enough stone to have built a wall right around France, 7ft (2m) high and 3ft (1m) thick. Not only that, but the stones are fitted together so accurately, and without cement, that there are only a few millimetres between them, leaving barely a space into which a credit card could be inserted. Khufu's pyramid covers a ground area of 13 acres (5

Detail showing the construction of the Great Pyramid, which would once have had a sparkling white limestone façade.

hectares), enough to engulf Westminster Abbey, St. Peter's Basilica in Rome and the great cathedrals of Milan and Florence. For 4,000 years the Great Pyramid was the tallest man-made structure on the planet.

Its positioning is no accident, sitting as it does exactly halfway between ancient Egypt's western and eastern boundaries. If one were to take a giant pair of compasses, one point set at the very centre of the pyramid, the upper quarter-circle bisecting both the eastern and western boundaries, it would exactly span the Nile delta. The four sides measure the same length, to within a tolerance of 2.3in (58mm), while the 13-acre base is level and flat to within 0.6in (15mm).

There are, in fact, generally accepted theories as to how the Great Pyramid was built, though estimates of the workforce needed to construct it vary from 14,000 to 300,000. However many workers there were, and the number at any one time would have varied greatly, according to the demands of the project and the time of year, a city sprang up to accommodate the pyramids, with its own facilities, such as brewery and bakeries. The site was levelled to a great degree of accuracy, probably by digging a grid of trenches, filling them with water, then gradually draining them, which would have made any humps and hollows immediately obvious. The precise alignment of the Great Pyramid's square base would have been laid out according to the position of the stars, primarily the Pole Star, with fine adjustments made after observing the midnight positions of other stars. Once a true north had been established, it would have been relatively simple for the positions of the remaining sides to have been fixed.

The limestone was quarried nearby, on the eastern bank of the Nile, the Tura quarries, where the excavation tunnels can still be seen, supplying the fine white stone. The stone was then shaped using simple tools – T-squares and plumb lines – before being cut to size with copper saws and chisels. It is generally accepted that the stones (each weighing 2.5 tons, though with special granite slabs of up to 80 tons) were dragged up onto massive external and possibly internal ramps, allowing stones to be placed both from the inside and out. Egyptologists have calculated that a block would have been placed every two minutes, which is an astonishing feat not only of logistics and organization but also of engineering. The building of the Great Pyramid would have taken 20 years, even at that rate, added to which would have been the time needed for the design, surveying and the levelling of the site.

There have been countless theories as to why the Great Pyramid was built, but the conventional view is that it was simply a vast tomb for the Pharaoh Khufu (Cheops). The presence of shafts, aligned with the stars, seems to support this, being the means by which the dead pharoah could ascend directly to heaven. When workmen first tunnelled into the pyramid in AD 820, they found the tombs completely sealed, indicating that no one had been there before them; yet neither the body of the pharaoh, nor those of his queen or the pall-bearers were found.

It is sometimes said that the pyramid was a grand diversionary tactic, and that the pharaoh's body was actually buried in a more modest tomb that would not attract grave robbers. That is possible, as is the view that the astronomer-priests who masterminded the Great Pyramid used its construction to perfect their knowledge of astronomy, mathematics and astrology, which would explain the pyramid's precise alignments and perfect dimensions. Whatever the truth and whatever the Great Pyramid's true purpose, nothing can detract from its scale, its grandeur, and the miracle of its construction.

THE NAZCA LINES

Erich von Daniken has a lot to answer for, in that his book, *The Chariots of the Gods*, created a huge following, being a great success worldwide with over five million copies sold and translated into 26 languages. Its

premise is that aliens visited the Earth about 10,000 years ago, creating 'intelligent man by altering the genes of monkeys in their image', a theory that was later completely discredited. His evidence was 'almost totally irrelevant – an insidious mixture of half-fact and half-truth that sometimes spills into

RIGHT: A pre-Inca design, etched into a Nazca hillside.

BELOW: Another of Nazca's evocative images: is it an astronaut, a spaceman, or merely a stylized picture of a human being?

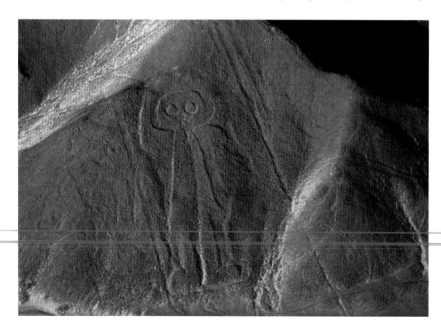

complete falsehood', according to Francis Hitching in *The World Atlas of Mysteries*.

Without von Daniken, however, it is unlikely that the Nazca lines would have become quite so well-known. Described by Hitching as 'the largest work of art in the world', these massive geoglyphs appear in the Nazca Desert, a 500-sq mile (1295-km^2) plateau in western Peru. Etched onto the ground are giant hummingbirds, fish, monkeys and spiders, lizards, insects and llamas, with straight lines radiating from some that are miles long, the largest figures being nearly 900ft (275m) long. They had been

OPPOSITE & BELOW: The secrets of the Nazca plateau remained safe until they were fully revealed from the air once aircraft began to fly over the area.

barely noticed at ground level until they were seen from the air in 1939 when aircraft began to fly over the area.

According to von Daniken, the Nazca lines had a specific purpose: 'At some time in the past, unknown intelligences landed on the uninhabited plain near the present-day town of Nazca and built an improvised airfield for their spacecraft which were to operate in the vicinity of the Earth. They laid down two runways on the ideal terrain.'

Like other theories in von Daniken's book, this was later debunked; not only is it unlikely that an advanced spacecraft would have needed a runway miles long, but as German archeologist and mathematician Dr. Maria Reiche pointed out, after having studied the Nazca lines for 25 years, the ground is too soft to support UFOs: 'The spacemen,' she contended, 'would have gotten stuck.'

But the Nazca lines remain a fascinating enigma, and it is still not

BELOW LEFT: What is possibly a tree of life with roots extending.

OPPOSITE: An exquisitely beautiful image of a condor.

precisely known how they were built or for what purpose. An early theory was that they are the remains of irrigation channels, the first scientist to examine them in detail being Dr. Paul Kosok, an agronomist from Long Island University. He first surveyed the figures in the 1930s, working out what each one represented, but came no closer to discovering their true purpose. But he realized why they had been scarcely noticeable before. They were very shallow indentations, made after removing the desert's thin layer of brown pebbles to reveal the lighter soil beneath. He wrote: 'Standing a few yards to the side makes a line invisible, but standing astride it makes the faintest line show clearly.'

In 1946 Kosok passed his research notes on to Dr. Reiche, who had a special interest in ancient sites. She would spend the next 25 years studying the lines, recording the exact dimensions of each figure, and become a world authority on the subject in the

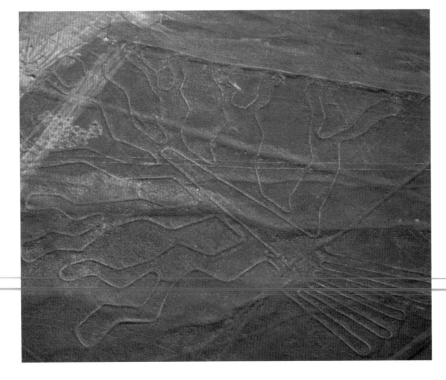

process. But she remained uncertain as to how such huge images could have been created over such large distances on the ground and still be so perfectly recognizable when viewed from ther air.

Bill Spohrer thought the constructors of the lines had some means by which they could check their creation from above, a theory which he sought to prove in 1975 by building a balloon out of the kind of materials that would have been available when the lines were laid out between 200 BC and AD 700. The fabric used was similar to an old piece of Nazcan cloth, which had a weave tighter than that of a modern parachute at 205 x 110 threads per square inch, and with a reed gondola carrying two men, the balloon was able to make a successful flight. More recent researchers, however, including Joe Nickell of the University of Kentucky, have succeeded in reproducing the figures on the ground using only simple tools.

As to why the lines were constructed, the question remains unanswered. It had been Maria Reiche's opinion that the lines were an astronomical calendar, indicating the rising of important stars and planetary events like the sun's solstices, although

astronomer Gerald Hawkins could find no evidence of this when he surveyed the lines in 1972. They could be religious symbols, made large so that only the gods could see them, or perhaps they were sacred paths, leading to sites where the gods could be worshipped?

Whatever their true purpose, the Nazca lines remain one of the wonders of the world, both as art and as a supreme feat of engineering.

MEGALITHIC ENGINEERING

The ancient Egyptians, Greeks and Romans had highly advanced civilizations, well versed in mathematics, astronomy and philosophy. They were good organizers and builders, too, able to construct and sustain great cities and promote long-distance trade with other nations. It was believed that the people of north-western Europe lagged far behind these mighty civilizations, and that while the Egyptians were building the pyramids, these northerners were living as primitive hunter-gatherers. The Romans built fine roads and magnificent aquaducts; the Britons painted themselves blue and were easy to conquer.

Stonehenge's great standing stones.

STRANGE PHENOMENA

This view of the people of Europe's northern fringes as barbarians was turned on its head when it was realized that the structures that they left behind – stone circles, standing stones and burial chambers – had been built methodically and with a great sense of purpose. The 600 or so stone circles in Britain had much in common with the pyramids and the civil engineering feats of the Romans, in that they required the marshalling of large numbers of people to transport heavy stones over long distances. In short, these

LEFT: The megalithic passage tomb at Newgrange, County Meath, Ireland, was built around 3200 BC.

BELOW: The tri-spiral design, seen at Newgrange, is probably the most famous of the Irish megalithic symbols.

megalithic monuments were planned, designed and built by intelligent, knowledgeable people.

The scale of their constructions were feats in themselves: Stonehenge's bluestones, some weighing four tons

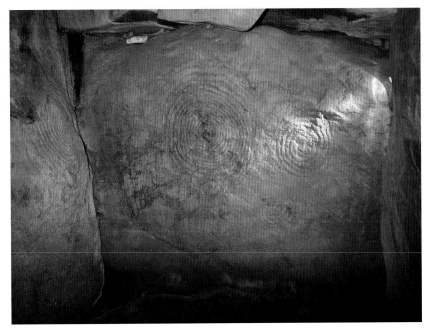

LEFT: There are three stone circles at Stanton Drew, Somerset, the Great Circle being one of the largest in the country.

OPPOSITE: The Callanish standing stones on Lewis, in the Outer Hebrides.

apiece, were brought 240 miles (390km) from the Preseli Mountains in Wales, partly by water and partly by dragging them overland on rollers and sledges. At Carnac, on the Atlantic coast of France, more than 3,000 standing stones are arranged in rows that stretch towards the horizon, and even these are thought to be but a small remaining part of a vast geometrical complex.

Unfortunately, it was the fate of many standing stones that they presented tempting and readily available sources of building material for subsequent generations.

In the early 18th century, antiquarians tended to dismiss the stones. 'All that can be learn'd of them,' wrote Daniel Defoe, 'is that they are.' Excavations around the stones revealed few clues as to their purpose, leading archeologists of the time to conclude that they were part of a primitive culture, the educated orthodoxy of the time being far more enamoured of the classical civilizations. As late as the 1920s, civilization was believed to have begun with the ancient Egyptians before spreading around the Mediterranean and beyond. Sir Mortimer Wheeler, President of the Society of Antiquities in London, believed that to attempt to link the stones with astronomy was a 'waste of time and ink'.

There were some, however, who had already recognized the astronomical connection: Sir J. Norman Lockyer (1836–1920), a British astronomer, a respected scientist of his day and the world's first professor of astronomical physics at the Royal College of Science, South Kensington, London (now part of Imperial College), noticed that many stone circles appeared to be aligned with the rising sun. His belief that ancient sites, such as Stonehenge, were axially oriented towards a place on the skyline where a celestial body – the sun, the moon, or a star – crossed the horizon on a particular day was developed by others, notably in around 1934 by Dr. Alexander Thom, later to be professor of engineering at Oxford University, who painstakingly surveyed some 300 megalithic circles, alignments and isolated standing stones in Britain. He discovered what he called the 'megalithic yard', a measurement of

2.72ft (0.83m) that was a recurring feature throughout the sites, and that the builders had used this and a knowledge of geometry to construct perfect ellipses and ovoids 1,000 years before Pythagoras. The dimensions of the right-angled triangles used implied that the builders had a knowledge of pi, or the numerical value of the ratio of the circumference of a circle to its diameter, indicating that although they were unable to read or write they were mathematicians nonetheless.

They were astronomers too: Newgrange, the impressive passage tomb in County Meath, Ireland, has its main passageway aligned so that the midwinter sun shines straight though it at sunrise, into a 'light box' at the far end. In fact, it was more complex than that: using markers on far horizons, the stone circles were in themselves observatories, built to detect the Moon's 'minor standstill', which occurs every 18.6 years, a small irregularity in the Moon's orbit which must have taken

decades, if not generations, of study to discover and accurately predict.

But the stones came to be viewed with suspicion by later generations. In early Christian times they were associated with the dark forces and with witchcraft, remnants of an age of pagan Sun worship. In southern England, from the Middle Ages onwards, a ceremony was held at the giant Avebury stone circle every 25

Castlerigg stone circle, Keswick, Cumbria.

years, in which one of the great stones would be felled and attacked to symbolize victory over the Devil. Maybe it was this early Christian association of the stones with paganism and primitive culture that led to conventional science ignoring their deeper meaning for so long.

Yet the sophisticated science underpinning the stones had been passed from generation to generation, without benefit of the written word, leading some to speculate how this had been achieved. They came to the conclusion that the ancient knowledge had become enshrined in epic verse, learned by heart by each new generation of the priesthood.

STONEHENGE

Stonehenge, sitting high on the chalk downland of Salisbury Plain in southern England, is probably the most important prehistoric monument in Britain, perhaps even in the whole of Europe. There are more extensive stone circles – at Castlerigg, Avebury and Stanton Drew – and some are more complete, but Stonehenge is the only raised stone circle, in that its massive lintels are supported on stones 15ft (4.6m) above the ground.

It is one of the oldest man-made constructions on Earth, the stonework alone having been evolved in several phases over 1,000 years. Its builders could neither read nor write, yet they planned and built this massive structure to a high degree of accuracy. Stonehenge is built on sloping ground, yet its circle of stones – 100ft (30m) across – are level and truly circular to within an inch or so. Now a World Heritage Site, it attracts around one million visitors every year.

There are many legends surrounding Stonehenge. In 1135, Geoffrey of Monmouth claimed that it had been brought from Africa, carried by a tribe of giants to Ireland before being transported to the Salisbury Plain by the wizard Merlin. Another legend also credits Merlin with erecting the stones on their present site, but indicates they were stolen from an Irishwoman by the Devil. But in 1130, Henry of Huntingdon had already given a more prosaic description, his being the earliest written account to survive: 'Stanenges, where stones of wonderful size have been erected after the manner of a doorway, so that doorway appears to have been raised upon doorway; and no one can conceive

how such great stones have been raised aloft, or why they were built there.'

A large earthwork, or a henge, once existed on Stonehenge's site, comprising a ditch, a bank and what are known as Aubrey holes, which are 3ft (1m) wide pits in the chalk, forming a circle 282ft (86m) across. Here, excavations revealed human bones, which were probably cremated at the bottom of these holes.

The henge was then abandoned for around 1,000 years until work began in 2150 BC on a new and far more dramatic and enduring structure. Eighty-two giant bluestones, quarried in the Preseli Mountains in south-west Wales, were transported to the Salisbury Plain, probably dragged on rollers and sledges to Milford Haven, then carried by water to England and up the rivers Avon and Frome. Back on land, they were then dragged to a site near what is now the town of Warminster, whence they were shipped up the Rivers Wylye and Salisbury Avon to Amesbury, just a couple of miles from Stonehenge. They were erected here in an incomplete double circle, at which time the Avenue was also built, being a pair of ditches 40ft (12m) apart and aligned with the midsummer sunrise. But this Stonehenge was quite unlike the one we

Stonehenge.

are familiar with today, the building of which had begun some 100 years earlier with the arrival of the giant sarsen stones. These hard, silicified sandstone rocks almost certainly came from the Marlborough Downs, a mere 25 miles (40km) north of Stonehenge. But there were no handy navigable rivers on which to float them to the site. The largest weighed 50 tons, and they had to be laboriously hauled overland, using rollers and sledges. It would have taken 500 men, hauling on leather ropes, to move each stone, with another 100 laying down rollers in front of sledges.

The stones were hauled into place on site as others were being transported, and were shaped with mauls or rounded stones, used as hand tools to pound the surfaces into shape. At least one modern re-enactment has demonstrated how the big stones were hauled upright by means of pits dug beneath them; a final stage of building after 1500 BC then saw the original bluestones rearranged in the shape we see today. Thirty sarsens, each weighing around 25 tons, had to be hauled upright in this way, but the far greater feat was the raising of the horizontal lintels to a position on top of

them, in a manner unique to Stonehenge. The lintels were then locked into place by means of both mortice-and-tenon and dovetail joints, making the 100-ft (30-m) circle, when it was complete, astonishingly accurate and level to within an inch, despite having been built on sloping ground.

After 1000 BC, Stonehenge was left to decline. It is thought that the Romans, when they arrived, may have destroyed part of it after the Druids opposed the Roman occupation, even though the Romans themselves were normally tolerant of local religions. But weather damage also played its part: sitting high on Salisbury Plain, Stonehenge is exposed to the prevailing south-westerly winds, toppling a stone in 1750 and another in 1797, while a gale in 1963 saw circle stone number 23 collapse to the ground. Visitors, too, have taken their toll, generations of them having chipped away at the stones to take home as souvenirs, which is the reason why they are no longer permitted to get within touching distance. Only the modern Druids are allowed to approach the stones at the summer solstice, thus allowing one of the oldest man-made structures on Earth to continue fulfilling its original purpose.

THE GREAT WALL OF CHINA

What are the largest man-made structures in the world? The ones that spring most readily to mind are all recent projects, with Taipei 101, the 1670-ft (509-m) pride of Taiwan, being undoubtedly the tallest (though towers that are taller still are under construction as we speak). In Holland, the Aalsmeer Flower Auction building claims to have the largest single floor area of any building, at almost 10,763,900sq ft (1000000m²). The biggest shopping mall in the USA, in Pennsylvania, goes by the name of the King of Prussia, though at 41,977,920sq ft (390000m²) it is dwarfed by the South China Mall, near Beijing, which is nearly twice the size. But surely the largest man-made structure of all is Boeing's gargantuan plant at Everett, Washington – all 13.3 cubic metres of it.

But it isn't. The largest, in terms of length, surface area and mass, is over 2,000 years old. The Great Wall of China is in places up to 26ft (8m) tall and stretches for 4,160 miles (6695km) from Shanhaiguan in the east to Lop Nur in the west, roughly tracing an arc along China's border with Inner Mongolia.

All of the above statistics refer to the current wall, built during the Ming Dynasty (1368–1644), but there were others before that. In fact there have been several, and the states of Qi, Zhao and Yan all built smaller walls to defend their borders. It was Qin Shi Huang, who unified China in 221 BC, who built the first national wall. To reinforce the new centralized regime, he ordered the destruction of the wall sections that divided his empire along the former state borders, replacing them with a new wall to defend his empire from the Xiongnu people north of the border. Stones from the mountains were used where the wall proceeded over mountain ranges, while rammed earth was utilized for construction in the plains, to save the considerable labour of transporting other materials. A massive labour force was nevertheless required to build Qin's wall, and it is thought that as many as a million people died in the process, buried inside the wall rather than given proper funerals.

Qin's wall was finished in around 200 BC but was repaired and rebuilt by succeeding dynasties; it was not until the 15th century, however, during the Ming Dynasty, that a new wall was

RIGHT & PAGES 98 & 99: The Great Wall of China, shown in some of its many aspects.

built further to the south to keep out the warring Mongols. Building technology had moved on since the Qin Dynasty, and the Ming wall was far stronger, build of bricks and stone throughout. The use of brick was significant, being a relatively new technology that enabled much faster building, although cut stones were still used for the foundations, the inner and outer brims and the gateways, because of their greater strength.

The finished structure was a great feat of engineering, and once again countless thousands of lives were sacrificed to its contruction, while at one time a million men were employed to guard its length. Seemingly regardless of the terrain, the wall marches over mountain-tops and across flat plains, its structure reflecting its intended military purpose; most of the wall's top is lined with battlements, with defensive gaps of about 9in (23cm) wide. Regular watchtowers were placed at intervals to house troops and weapons, as well as for relaying smoke signals along the length of the wall.

The wall was evidently an important means of communication as well as defence, and helped to defend the Chinese empire well after the Ming Dynasty had gone. It wasn't until 1644 that the Manchus were able to cross the Great Wall, and then only because the gates at Shanhaiguan had been opened by a Ming general with a hatred of the current Shun Dynasty.

But the Manchus, as the new rulers, had less use for the wall than their predecessors, chiefly because they had annexed Mongolia, though they did build a southern wall to protect the empire from the Miao people.

Dramatic and extensive as it is, the Great Wall of China has never been visible from space with the naked eye, although the idea was widely circulated and believed. In fact, the only way this can happen is by means of radar imaging. Such images were acquired by the Spaceborne Imaging Radar-C/X-Band Synthetic Aperture Radar (SIR-C/X-SAR), onboard the space shuttle *Endeavour* on 10 April 1994. They show two segments of the Great Wall of China in a desert region of north-central China, about 434 miles (700km) west of Beijing. The wall appears as a thin orange band, running from the top to the bottom of the left image, and from the middle upper-left to the lower-right of the right image.

Another Great Wall myth, and one that possibly just as many people believed at the time, was the alleged plan to demolish the wall in order to build a road. This surfaced in Denver, Colorado, in 1899, the story being that a group of American businessmen were heading off to China to seal the deal. The story was picked up by newspapers across the USA and Europe, but turned out to be a hoax, dreamed up by four Denver reporters on a day when real news was in short supply. In 1939, Denver songwriter, Harry Lee Wilber, claimed that the hoax was responsible for starting the Boxer Rebellion (1899–1901), but that too was a fabrication.

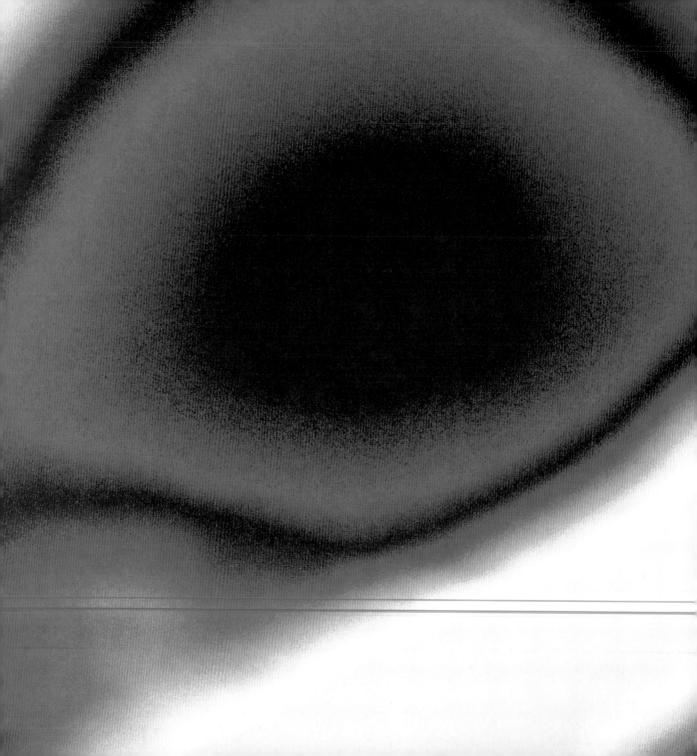

INTO
THIN AIR

The Mary Celeste
The Bermuda Triangle

CHAPTER FOUR
INTO THIN AIR

THE *MARY CELESTE*

The most famous sea mystery of all time remains just that – a mystery. There have been countless theories and explanations as to why this ordinary cargo ship was discovered, completely deserted, in the Atlantic Ocean in November 1872. What we do know is that the *Mary Celeste* left New York heading for Genoa, with Captain Briggs in command. He was an experienced sailor, a religious man who took his wife and two-year-old daughter on board, as well as a crew of eight, which he said in a letter before setting sail that he considered reliable.

A month later, the *Mary Celeste* was found by another ship, about 600 miles (965km) west of Gibraltar. Her sails were in place, but she had been moving so erratically that a boarding party was sent to investigate. There was no one on board and the only lifeboat was missing. Everything was in good order, and toys were found on the captain's bed, as if his daughter had been playing there before there had been a hurried exit. But there was no sign of any struggle, and in spite of there being 3ft (1m) of water in the hold, the *Mary Celeste* was still completely seaworthy. Her cargo – 1,700 barrels of commercial alcohol – was intact, and had been well-insured. There were provisions for six months in the stores, and a good supply of fresh water. What had caused the entire crew to have abandoned ship so suddenly? Could something more sinister have befallen her?

LEFT: An engraving of the ill-fated Mary Celeste.

OPPOSITE: A tall ship, reminiscent of the Mary Celeste, *sailing at sunset.*

She was certainly regarded as an unlucky ship, if not a jinxed one. Built in 1861 in Nova Scotia and named *The Amazon*, her first captain had died a few days after she was registered. Her second master, on her maiden voyage with him, was dismissed for incompetence after she had been run into a fishing weir and a fire had broken out during repairs. The following year she made it across the Atlantic, but collided with a brig in the Straits of Dover, suffering serious damage while the other ship sank. Then, four years later, she ran aground on Cape Breton Island and was declared a wreck before being salvaged and renamed the *Mary Celeste*. The man who saved her, Alexander McBean, became bankrupt, and the ship passed through the hands of two more owners before setting sail from New York under her fifth captain, Benjamin Spooner Briggs.

So what happened? Possible scenarios (if we exclude abduction by aliens or sea monsters) come under three headings: violence, illness or a crisis of some kind. The official explanation, from the US Secretary of the Treasury, William A. Richard, comes under the first heading, and was

that the crew had imbibed some of the alcoholic cargo and had murdered the captain and his family while drunk. When the *Mary Celeste* was found, several sailors came forward, claiming to be 'sole survivors' of the ship (though none was on the crew register): a Mr. Trigg told how the crew had found a derelict treasure ship and had abandoned their own; a Mr. Pemberton listed horrific killings, nightmarish storms and strange delusions; and Abel

Fosdyk explained that everyone was crowded onto a platform on the ship's bows, watching a swimming race between the ship's captain and a crew member, when the platform collapsed and they all fell into the sea to be eaten by sharks.

There are numerous other explanations, many no less fanciful: that the crew of the ship that had discovered the *Mary Celeste* were responsible for hijacking it and killing

the crew; that Captain Briggs murdered everyone while in the grip of religious delusions; or that everyone had been driven mad by a cloud of poisonous gas or by bad bread (the fungus ergot can infect rye bread, causing delusions and suicidal tendencies). But there are convincing reasons why all of these explanations (and others) are highly unlikely, perhaps the most feasible being the one put forward by Oliver Deveau at the inquiry, which was that the *Mary Celeste*, though not in danger, did have water in the hold, making it possible that someone mistakenly thought she was sinking and sounded the alarm. But whatever the occurrence, none of the crew, nor the lifeboat, was ever seen again.

The *Mary Celeste* continued her eventful career. Back in New York, under a new owner and captain, she set sail for Montevideo with a cargo of lumber, when a severe storm swept the entire deck cargo overboard, destroying much of the rigging. Repaired, and now with a cargo of horses, the ship set sail once more, but most of the livestock died en route, followed by the captain a few days later. Then, after an uneventful few years, she was bought by Gilman C. Parker, who deliberately

grounded her on a coral reef, sprinkled her with kerosene and set fire to her in order to claim the insurance. The scam was discovered, but with insufficient evidence Parker and his cronies were released. The two companies involved went bankrupt.

THE BERMUDA TRIANGLE

It is easy to be sceptical about the Bermuda Triangle which, according to authors Janet and Colin Bord, is neither a triangle nor concentrated on

OPPOSITE: Numerous books have been written on the mysterious subject of the Bermuda Triangle.

BELOW: Could missing ships have been sucked into a giant whirlpool?

Bermuda. Indeed some have extended this area of strange happenings out as far east as the Azores, which turns it into a vast trapezium stretching right out into the Atlantic Ocean. According to Lawrence Kusche, a research

librarian at Arizona State University, whose book sought to debunk the whole idea: 'The legend of the Bermuda Triangle is a manufactured mystery…perpetuated by writers who either purposely or unknowingly made use of misconceptions, faulty reasoning and sensationalism.'

That ships, boats and planes have gone missing in the area is undisputed. A celebrated case is that of Flight 19, a training mission of TBM Avenger bombers that disappeared without trace on 5 December 1945. The flight was led by an experienced pilot, Lt. Charles Carroll Taylor, and the weather was calm. Some accounts imply that the aircrafts' compasses had been sent awry by strange magnetic forces, or that the pilots had encountered some other unusual phenomenon, while the US Navy's official report put the disappearance down to 'causes or reasons unknown'.

It is also thought that Taylor's mother influenced the report's conclusion to save her son's reputation. Although he was the most experienced pilot on the mission, in fact the only one with significant flying hours to his credit, Taylor had a history of becoming lost in the air, having done so three times during the Second World War when his aircraft had to be ditched twice. On that fateful day in December 1945 Taylor is thought to have been 30

miles (48km) north-west of where he believed himself to be, while written records of radio conversations between Taylor and the other pilots make no

OPPOSITE: The USS Cyclops *disappeared without trace en route to Baltimore on 4 March 1918, after making an unscheduled stop at Barbados. No wreckage was ever found.*

ABOVE: The Panamanian Sylvia L. Ossa *is shown after docking at New Orleans in March 1975. The 590-ft (180-m) cargo ship, with her 37 crew, was reported lost in the infamous Bermuda Triangle the following year and no trace of her or her crew was ever found.*

mention of suspect compass readings. Finally, while the flight had set out in good weather, it had begun to get stormy by the time of its disappearance.

In March 1918, the naval cargo ship, USS *Cyclops*, disappeared, complete with her crew of 306, though it is thought that storms or enemy activity may have had something to do with this; there was war with Germany at the time, and German submarines were active in the Atlantic.

Then there was the case of the *Teignmouth Electron*, which bears something of a resemblance to a classic Bermuda Triangle story. The trimaran had been heading for home after a gruelling round-the-world yacht race in

1969, when it was found abandoned, the craft afloat and undamaged. This was puzzling, for if Donald Crowhurst, its lone skipper, had only kept on going he would have been on course for an enthusiastic welcome on reaching home. A little research reveals a very different reality, however, in that Crowhurst appears to have had very limited experience of long-distance sailing, unlike the professionals against whom he was competing. Already under financial pressure before he even started the race, he nevertheless decided to go ahead, leaving his wife and family behind. Then, unaccountably, he decided to turn back before his inadequate trimaran had even left the Atlantic Ocean. His plan, as later revealed in his written log, was to hole up in the Atlantic and wait there, then to follow the leading yachts on the home stretch, giving the impression he had also sailed around the world single-handed. The log also reveals how he was becoming increasingly irrational, and it is thought that, burdened by guilt and fear of being found out, he committed suicide by throwing himself overboard.

According to the US Coastguard, boats certainly do get into trouble in the Bermuda Triangle, but no more than anywhere else, and in fact proportionately less so considering the high level of traffic passing through the area. In 1975, the service recorded 21 vessels lost without trace off the US coast, but only four of these were in the triangle. And there are good reasons why ships should founder here: the Gulf Stream flows through the area at 5-6 knots, sudden storms are liable to blow up, and hurricanes are common during both the summer and autumn. In spite of this, Lloyds of London, the insurance giant, does not consider it a risk worse than any other stretch of water, and does not charge higher premiums for ships crossing it.

Human error, so often a major cause of accident, on land as well as on sea, is another factor. On examining the apparently mysterious explosion aboard the VA *Fogg* in 1972, the US Coast Guard concluded the most likely cause to have been the lack of training given to crew engaged in cleaning out the volatile benzene residue in the ship's tanks. As for the complete disappearance of wreckage and bodies, the strong and steady Gulf Stream is likely to have made a good job of dispersing them well out into the vast Atlantic Ocean.

Lawrence Kusche examined 43 such cases of disappearances in the triangle and concluded that almost every one of them could be explained. The schooner *Gloria Colita*, for example, was in 1940 found mysteriously abandoned in the Gulf of Mexico in calm weather. He checked a newspaper report of the incident, which revealed that severe storms had been hitting the area and that far from being in good order 'the rigging was in shreds and her rudder and steering apparatus shattered…the hold was nearly filled with water'.

BELOW & OPPOSITE: Could it be that natural forces, common to the Gulf of Mexico and beyond, go a long way to explain these sudden disappearances?

Perhaps the lesson to be learned is that everyone enjoys the frisson to be had from a good mystery, and tales of the Bermuda Triangle are no exception. Or to be more cynical is to realize that mysteries and the paranormal are always popular subjects for books – and can be highly profitable as far as their authors are concerned.

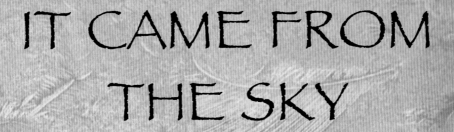

IT CAME FROM THE SKY

Meteors and their Craters

The Devastation of Siberia

It's Raining Cats & Dogs

UFOs

Phantom Armies

CHAPTER FIVE

IT CAME FROM THE SKY

METEORS AND THEIR CRATERS

Two hundred million meteorites enter the Earth's atmosphere every day, which would be a recipe for daily global disaster if the vast majority did not disintegrate long before they hit the ground. These are what we see as shooting stars, and it is thought that some 500 a year do make it to the ground, of which only 1 per cent is ever recovered. Most are tiny, but the biggest have been responsible for global changes, including (though this is still debated) the extinction of the dinosaurs. The largest meteoritic crater in the world, at Vredefort in South Africa, is 180 miles (290km) in

BELOW: Wolf Creek Crater, Great Sandy Desert, Western Australia.

OPPOSITE: Gosse Bluff Crater, the Tnorala Convervation Reserve, Australia.

THE TEN BIGGEST METOR CRATERS

Vredefort, South Africa
180 miles (290km) diameter

Sudbury Basin, Canada
156 miles (250km) diameter

Chicxulub, Mexico
110 miles (177km) diameter

Manicouagan Reservoir, Canada
62 miles (100km) diameter

Popigai, Siberia, Russia
62 miles (100km) diameter

Acraman, Australia
56 miles (90km) diameter

Chesapeake Bay
56 miles (90km) diameter

Mjolnir, Barents Sea
25 miles (40km) diameter

Mason, USA
24 miles (39km) diameter

Clearwater Lakes, Canada
twin craters, 16 and 23 miles (26 and 37km) diameter

diameter, having been formed when a meteor, perhaps 6 miles (10km) across, hit the ground at a hypervelocity of over 6,700mph (10780km/h)

For nearly 2,000 years, scientific orthodoxy insisted that meteors did not come from space, but was matter carried up from the Earth's surface by strong winds which later fell back to the ground. Aristotle firmly believed this, and that the shooting stars seen from the Earth were more akin to rainbows than solid objects. As late as 1807, US President Thomas Jefferson, himself a scientist, on hearing that two Yale University professors had weighed 300lb (136kg) of meteorites that had fallen on Connecticut during December declared: 'It is easier to believe that two Yankee Professors would lie, than that stones would fall from heaven.' But Jefferson's remarks was soon to be made trivial by events, and by 1820 it was generally accepted in the scientific community that meteors were solid, and that they came from space.

Most meteors are chondrites, composed of silicate material from the asteroid belt, thought to be around 4.5 billion years old. A far smaller proportion, about 8 per cent, are achondrites, similar to the igneous rocks found on earth, and about 5 per cent are iron, including iron-nickel alloys, freed perhaps from the core of asteroids after collision with others of their kind. Iron meteroids, better able to survive the burning rush down through the Earth's atmosphere, are more likely to hit ground, and far larger stony or icy bodies usually break up long before. Shooting stars are highly visible at night, and meteors are rarely seen by day. However, there have been reported sightings of bright fireballs, with flashes and bursts of light becoming visible as the meteor breaks up. Sonic booms have also been heard during meteoritic falls, sometimes over a very wide area.

Of the few meteors that do reach ground, how many people or animals have been hit by them? There have been several reports, not all credible or well-documented. A dog was reportedly killed by a meteorite in Egypt in 1911, and there are unsubstantiated reports of a cow and a horse having been killed since then. We do know that the home of Ann Hodges, of Sylacauga, Alabama, was hit by a 9-lb (4-kg) stone chondrite meteor in November 1954; this crashed through the roof of her house, bouncing off the living-room radio set and striking Mrs. Hodges, who was taken to hospital suffering from severe bruising.

But that which hit Ann Hodges was a pygmy compared with the meteors that hit the Earth, with catastrophic results, in prehistoric times. The Chicxulub Crater, buried beneath the Yucutan Peninsula in Mexico, is over 110 miles (177km) in diameter, the asteroid which caused it having been at least 6 miles (10km) in diameter. Dated to the late Cretaceous period, about 65 million years ago, the Chicxulub meteor has long been associated with the sudden extinction of the dinosaurs. Not all scientists agree, however, though many accept it as a possible contributory factor.

The scale of the hit would have been astonishing, in that a meteor of this size, hitting the Earth at hypervelocity, would have released an energy equivalent of 100 teratons of TNT, or be about two million times more powerful than the most potent man-made bomb. The impact would have set off megatsunamis, and pieces of the meteor would have shot back up into space, beyond the atmosphere, only to fall back as burning meteors, igniting huge wildfires on Earth.

The shock waves of the impact would have caused earthquakes and volcanic eruptions all over the globe, and enough dust and particles would have been emitted to have covered the entire surface of the Earth for as much as ten years. That would have made it difficult enough for life to survive, but huge amounts of carbon dioxide, caused by the destruction of carbonate rocks, would have created an intense greenhouse effect, while dust particles in the atmosphere would have filtered out sunlight, stunting plant growth. The effects would have been so

An aeriel view, taken from space, of what is now the Manicouagan Reservoir in central Québec, the fourth largest crater on earth. The meteor impact is thought to have occurred about 215 million years ago, towards the end of the Triassic period, and may have been responsible for the extinction of roughly 60 per cent of the living species of that time.

monstrous and far-reaching that the entire food chain would have been irrevocably disrupted.

Could a single meteor really have been the cause of all this? Not everyone

agrees, but it is certain that meteors will continue to hit the Earth, although we would have to be extremely unlucky to experience another Chicxulub.

DEVASTATION IN SIBERIA

The Tunguska Basin, deep in the Siberian interior, is one of the most remote places on Earth, and was even more so in pre-revolutionary Russia, when the sparse population of nomads and peasants witnessed a devastating explosion, equivalent to 10–20 megatons of TNT and 1,000 times more powerful than the atomic bomb dropped on Hiroshima. But this happened on 30 June 1908, when such weapons were as yet unknown, so what was the Tunguska explosion, what caused it, and what kind of effect did it leave behind?

It is hardly surprising that some people thought they were witnessing the end of the world. It was around

ABOVE: The huge meteorite, known as Tungus, fell on this spot in Siberia in 1908.

OPPOSITE ABOVE: Leonid Kulik, a Russian researcher, led an expedition to investigate the impact of the meteorite reponsible for devastating Tunguska.

OPPOSITE BELOW: The aftermath of the impact.

There was so much heat that I was no longer able to remain where I was – my shirt almost burned off my back. I saw a huge fireball that covered an enormous part of the sky. I only had a moment to note the size of it. Afterwards it became dark and at the same time I felt an explosion that threw me several feet from the porch. I lost consciousness for a few moments and when I came to I heard a noise that shook the whole house and nearly moved it off its foundations.'

In 1926, I.M. Suslov recorded this account taken from the Chuchan of the Shanyagir tribe: 'The Earth began to move and rock, wind hit our hut and knocked it over. My body was pushed

7.15am that settlers near Lake Baikal saw a column of light in the sky, which they later described as nearly as bright as the sun. About ten minutes later came a loud noise, some said like artillery fire, along with a shock wave so strong that windows were shattered hundreds of miles away. Closer to the event, the consequences were far more catastrophic. A farmer described what he saw, sitting on the porch of his house, just 40 miles (64km) away: 'There appeared a great flash of light.

down by sticks, but my head was in the clear. Then I saw a wonder: trees were falling, the branches were on fire, it became mighty bright, how can I say this, as if there was a second sun, my eyes were hurting, I even closed them. It was like what the Russians call lightning. And immediately there was a loud thunderclap. This was the second thunder. The morning was sunny, there were no clouds, our Sun was shining brightly as usual, and suddenly there came a second one!… We looked at the fallen trees, watched the treetops get snapped off, watched the fires.'

These eyewitness accounts paint only a small part of the picture. Eighty million trees were felled over an area of 800sq miles (2072km²), and an oval-shaped area around the explosion was completely devastated. With temperatures at millions of degrees Centigrade, the seismic effect measured 5.0 on the Richter scale.

What exactly happened on this summer morning in Siberia remained a mystery for many years, partly because of the remoteness of the location, partly because Russia was plunged into the chaos of revolution and civil war within a few years. Not until 1927, 19 years after the event, did minerologist

Leonid Kulik mount an expedition to the area. He was expecting to find a massive crater, but there was nothing of the sort. Inevitably, a number of alternative theories were posited, some believing the disaster to have been caused by a 'small' (1020- to 1022-g) black hole passing through the Earth, while others thought a comet passing through the Earth's atmosphere would have had the same effect. Unfortunately for the black hole theory there is no evidence of a so-called 'exit event', i.e., a second explosion occurring as the black hole, having tunnelled through the Earth, shot out of its other side on its way back into space. Then, of course, came the UFO theories, one being that Tunguska was simply the site where a UFO had crashed to Earth.

Today, the explanation most widely accepted is that a meteoroid or a piece of a comet exploded 3–6 miles (5–10km) above the surface of the Earth; most meteors burn up or explode in the atmosphere before they reach the surface, although never since on this scale. Such an airburst would have caused the effects suffered by Tunguska and its inhabitants without leaving a crater. One puzzle is that although millions of trees were torn up,

those closest to the centre remained upright. Atmospheric nuclear tests in the 1950s revealed the explanation: at ground zero the force was vertical, fanning out horizontally after hitting the ground.

Perhaps the most sobering aspect of the Tunguska explosion is what would have happened if it had occurred over a densely populated area. According to the *Guinness Book of Records*, if it had occurred 4 hours and 47 minutes later, it would have been right over St. Petersburg, which would have been completely destroyed.

IT'S RAINING CATS AND DOGS!

'It's raining men,' went the Weather Girls' international hit of 1982, but far stranger things have fallen out of the sky, including mice, snakes, rats, toads, larvae, grains, and lumps of flesh, as well as frogs and fishes. There have also been larger animals too: alligators have been known, and there was even a case of a cow falling from above. There are so many accounts of these strange incidences, occurring right up to modern times, that they cannot all have been hoaxes, and there are nearly as many explanations. No one, however,

Gibraltar, where millions of frogs are reputed to have fallen from the sky onto the rock in around 1915.

has been able to get to the bottom of this strange phenomenon.

Some of the earliest accounts date back to the ancient Greeks, when in around AD 200 Anentaeus summarized writings on the subject found in the Great Library of Alexandria. 'Phaenias, for example, says, in the second book of The Rulers of Eresus that in Chersonesus it rained fishes for three whole days. And Phylarcus in his fourth book says that certain persons have in many places seen it rain fishes, and the same thing with tadpoles.' But fast forward to 1859 and a storm over the village of Mountain Ash, in Wales, deposited 'thousands' of living fish. They were small, between 1 and 4in (2.5 and 10cm) long, the two showers occurring solely within the vicinity of a lumber yard. Charles Fort, a New Yorker who investigated strange phenomena in the early 20th century, drily observed that 'someone doused someone else with a pail full of water in which were thousands of fishes, some of which covered roofs of houses'.

Small frogs are a recurring theme in these strange events. Tens of thousands of them are reported to have fallen during a storm in Brignoles, France, in September 1973, while 'millions' had fallen over Gibraltar 58 years earlier. It is said that the English seaside town of Bournemouth suffered a violent thunderstorm in 1891, accompanied, according to an eyewitness report, published in *English Mechanic* magazine 20 years later, by a fall of tiny frogs. The man took shelter and saw 'small yellow frogs dashed on the ground all around me…[and]… thousands impaled on the furze bushes on the common close by'. In fact, Britain seems to be a favourite place for raining fish and frogs, for in the recent past, fish have been found stranded on a roof in London, in the seaside resort of Great Yarmouth, and in Stroud, Gloucestershire.

The only thing stranger than raining small animals is the raining of larger ones, though accounts of these are comparatively rare. Oddest of all (though it turned out to have a logical explanation) was the case of the falling cow. A Soviet ship in the Pacific spotted an upturned boat, rescuing the only survivor who babbled that the boat had been hit by a cow. The poor man was written off as insane and was carted off to a mental hospital; but one of the rescuers decided to take a further look. He discovered that a supply plane had been flying overhead, with a cow in its cargo bay. The creature broke free, and when the crew was unable to restrain it, it was dumped

ABOVE: The English seaside town of Bournemouth suffered a violent thunderstorm in 1891, accompanied, according to an eyewitness report, by a fall of tiny frogs.

OPPOSITE: There have even been reports of it raining rats.

out of the open hatch, making the boat that broke its fall unlucky for being in the right place at the wrong time.

So how can these strange rains be explained away? Creationism, or 'spontaneous generation', has it that small animals simply came into being in the air, fully formed, and from there fell to Earth, while teleportation (of which Charles Fort was also an adherent) suggests that animals 'flew' through the air before falling from an appearing

point. A more science-based theory, however, is that fish found in unexpected places may have been regurgitated by birds, but unless entire flocks have a tendency to do this simultaneously, it still does not explain the phenomenon.

The most credible modern explanation is that whirlwinds or waterspouts have the power to suck up small animals (fish and frogs especially) into the sky, carrying them through the air and depositing them elsewhere. But

there are problems even with this apparently logical explanation: if frogs from freshwater ponds were gathered up by waterspouts, why not tadpoles and pond weed as well, but there has never been any mention of these. Moreover, there are far more tornadoes in lake-rich Minnesota than there are in Britain, but no falls of fish, while there are accounts of frogs or fish falling from a clear blue sky. While many falls can be explained by storms, how is it that, according to

so many accounts, the animals survive falls of thousands of feet? One is left with the feeling that some of these phenomena have never been fully explained away by science.

UFOs

Kenneth Arnold was blissfully unaware of the controversy he was about to start, at least, not at the time. On 24 June 1947 he was piloting a plane over the Cascade Mountains of Washington state when he thought he saw something strange sharing his airspace. He later described seeing several shining craft, moving like 'saucers skipping over the water'. The world's press quickly latched on to the idea of 'flying saucers', which became a regular feature of newspaper reports throughout the 1950s, '60s, '70s and beyond. Were these unidentified lights in the sky simply stars, or planes that should never have been there, or were they advanced aircraft emanating from far-off galaxies?

Two weeks after Kenneth Arnold had made his report, the controversy was stepped up a gear when an

A fake photograph of an Unidentified Flying Object (UFO).

taking place and that the US military knew about UFOs but was refusing to divulge the truth. Since then, the incident has turned into a worldwide pop culture phenomenon, and Roswell ranks as the most famous site of alleged UFO landings.

Conspiracy theories aside, do UFOs actually exist? The short answer is yes, of course they do, but because these objects cannot be positively identified does not automatically mean they are from another world.

LEFT: Seen at Val Camonica, now a UNESCO World Heritage Site in alpine Italy, is a prehistoric rock carving of a figure which has long been known as 'the astronaut'.

BELOW: Farmer Edwin Fuhr indicates the spot where his rapeseed crop was flattened by five UFOs, as they hovered over his field near Langenburg, Saskatchewan, Canada, on 10 September 1974.

incident occurred near Roswell Army Air Field in New Mexico, on 8 July, the details of which are contradictory to say the least. Some say that the USAAF spokesman, when he reported that a flying saucer had crashed, producing 'material' to back this up, was joking in an attempt to divert attention from the top-secret projects going on at Roswell.

But the USAAF then denied the story, claiming that the incident involved the recovery of one of its balloons, which only served to reinforce the view that a sinister cover-up was

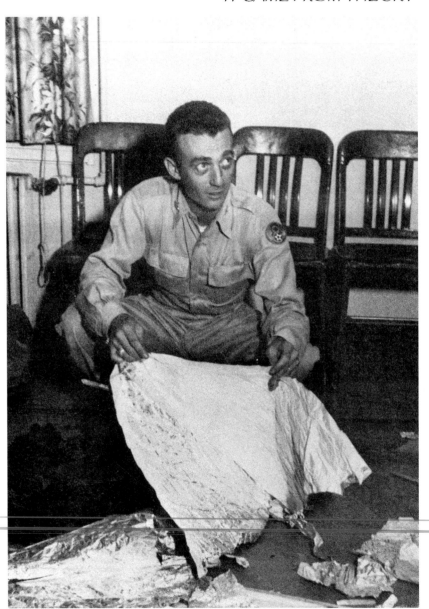

On 8 July 1947, the Roswell Army Air Field (RAAF), New Mexico, issued a press release reporting that the USAAF 509th Bomb Group had recovered a crashed 'flying disc' from a ranch nearby, sparking intense media interest. Later that day came a conflicting statement that it was a weather balloon that had in fact been recovered, rather than a flying saucer. In 1978, ufologist Stanton T. Friedman interviewed Major Jesse Marcel, who had been part of the original recovery team in 1947, whose belief it was that the recovery of an alien spacecraft had been covered up.

LEFT: Major Jesse Marcel, photographed in 1947, holds the tattered remains of recovered material which, to him, seemed to be 'not of this earth'.

ABOVE: The front page of the Roswell Daily Record from 9 July 1947.

Hanger 84, at what was once the Roswell Army Air Field, where the remains of UFO wreckage and alien bodies from the 1947 Roswell incident were allegedly stored.

There has certainly been no lack of sightings. A 1974 Gallup poll found that 11 per cent of US citizens claimed to have seen UFOs, while J. Allen Hynek (a consultant to the USAF's UFO investigations, from which he later dissociated himself) reported that an average 20 per cent of his lecture audiences raised their hands when the same question was asked. Writer John Keel, also keen to investigate, subscribed to a press cuttings service and was soon receiving 150 reports of sightings a day, with over 10,000 in 1966.

Stories of alien abductions are also relatively common, if citizens of the USA are to be believed. A 1991 poll by the Roper organization asked that particular question, its figures extrapolated across the entire population, which indicated that 2 per cent – that's five million people – claimed to have been abducted by aliens at some point in their lives. French astrophysicist Jacques Vallée estimated that taking non-reported incidents into account, and the fact that most sightings happen at night when

IT CAME FROM THE SKY

LEFT: An artist's impression of the infamous Men in Black, purported to visit witnesses at the time of UFO sightings. They sometimes have glowing eyes or other monstrous features, and claim to be government agents, who then proceed to harass or threaten UFO witnesses into maintaining silence. 'All MIB are not necessarily garbed in dark suits,' says American writer, Jerome Clark. 'The term is a generic one, used to refer to any unusual, threatening or strangely behaved individual whose appearance on the scene can be linked in some fashion with a UFO sighting'.

OPPOSITE ABOVE LEFT: A UFO, photographed by 17-year-old Alexander Pavlov, accompanied by a witness, and seen over the Volga river in Tver, Russia, in 1991.

OPPOSITE BELOW LEFT: A UFO, photographed by Augusto Arrando at Yungay, Peru, in March 1967.

OPPOSITE RIGHT: Pascagoula, Mississippi: an artist's impression of an alien seen by an abductee in October 1973.

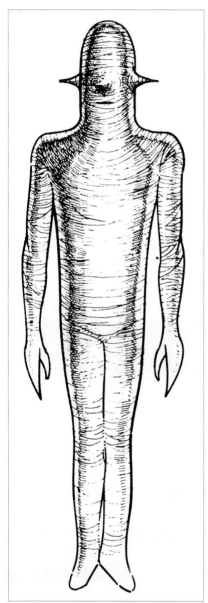

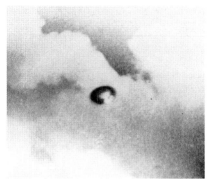

fewer people are around to see them, there should have been as many as three million landings in the 1950s, '60s and early '70s.

This is clearly nonsense, and serious research groups into UFOs agree that the vast majority of sightings are in fact IFOs – Identifiable Flying Objects. The Ground Saucer Watch at Phoenix, Arizona, lists 109 objects that could be mistaken for extraterrestrial

LEFT: A UFO, photographed by George J. Stock at Passaic, New Jersey, on 29 July 1952.

ABOVE: UFO photographed by Elizabeth Klarer in South Africa in the 1950s.

OPPOSITE: A note with a message in alien script, found at a UFO landing site by Robert Milcher of Tampa, Florida.

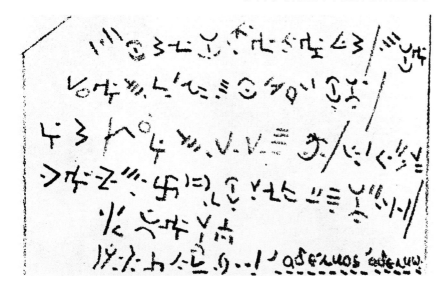

were a million other advanced civilizations in the galaxy, each sending out a spaceship every year and visiting 10 per cent of all the stars therein, Earth could only expect one visit every 10,000 years.

So the likelihood of UFO sightings, landings and abductions being true seems slim, to say the least, but our continuing fascination with the subject, if not still at the popular science-fiction peak of the 1950s, remains, with the sneaking feeling that, however unlikely UFOs may seem, we just don't know either way for sure.

PHANTOM ARMIES

Anyone who has seen the last film in the *Lord of the Rings* trilogy will surely remember the climactic scene when, at a critical point of the battle, a spectral army joins the fray, helping to secure an ultimate victory for the good guys. Phantom armies, coming to the aid of anyone from 11th-century Crusaders to British infantrymen in the trenches of the First World War, are a recurrent theme, usually seen fighting for what can be regarded as a just cause.

A classic example dates from 1537, from outside the city of Otranto, in southern Italy, then being attacked

craft, and includes fireflies, satellites and the planet Venus. According to Francis Hitching (*The World Atlas of Mysteries*) only 1 or 2 per cent of UFO sightings cannot be explained away.

Does this mean that life could well exist in other galaxies? The idea was given more credence in the 1990s, when biologists discovered nanobacteria that could exist in highly toxic or hostile environments – the sorts of places in which life had previously been thought impossible. These bacteria are also small enough to travel through space on the debris of meteors.

There is a large difference, however, between tough little bacteria and the existence of civilizations advanced enough to send spaceships vast distances across the galaxies. Alpha Centauri is the nearest star system to ours with the potential for supporting life. According to Philip J. Klass, once the editor of *Aviation Week & Space Technology* and the author of seven books debunking UFOs, it would take its inhabitants 50 years to reach Earth, even if their craft could cruise at 70 million miles per hour – the speed of light. By the same comparison, the same craft would take only 1.2 seconds to travel from the Earth to the Moon at that speed. Author Ian Ridpath, writing in the *New Scientist* journal, speculated that even if there by a Turkish army commanded by Suleiman the Magnificent. Fifty-seven years earlier, an attack by Mehmed II had left 800 men dead while defending the city, but according to an early Christian bishop of Otranto, their unburied bodies showed neither the signs of decay after 13 months in the open, nor did birds or animals attempt to eat them. Contemporary accounts have it that these 800 'martyrs' reappeared at the later battle, accompanied by angels, helping the people of Otranto in their task of defeating the Turks. They did the same in 1644, when another Ottoman attack was similarly beaten off.

Two years earlier, the maelstrom of the English Civil War, fought between the Royalist forces of King Charles I and the Parliamentarian army, commanded by the Earl of Essex, gave rise to two reports of phantom armies, separated by a few weeks in different parts of the country. At 5pm on 4 August 1642, while nothing was apparently to be seen, the sounds of a fierce battle could be heard, apparently being fought in the skies over Aldeburgh, in England. According to a pamphlet of the time, there was 'the beating of Drums, the discharging of

Muskets and great Ordnance for the space of an hour or more', added to which was the fact that 'many men of good worth' heard this symphony of

destruction and were prepared to testify as much in the House of Commons. In the midst of all this, a great stone is said to have fallen out of the sky.

OPPOSITE: A woodcut from 1680 of a vision of a phantom army.

RIGHT: Aldeburgh, where on 4 August 1642 the sounds of a raging battle were clearly heard but not seen.

A few weeks later the Battle of Edge Hill, fought in Warwickshire, was the first pitched battle of the English Civil War. For four successive Saturday and Sunday nights, the battle was re-enacted in the sky, and again there were respectable witnesses willing to swear that what they had seen was true. Once again, a pamphlet was produced to publicize the story: 'A great Wonder in Heaven, shewing the late Apparitions and Prodigious Noyse of War and Battels seene on Edge-Hill, neere Keinton, in Warwickshire, 1642.'

In such tumultuous times, when families and friends were being set one against the other, it could be argued that what the witnesses were experiencing was mass hallucination, similar to a crowd witnessing the Indian rope trick. One can also imagine a foot soldier on the ground in a desperate situation, charged with adrenalin, who looks up and sees what he desperately wants to see.

In fact, all sorts of explanations have been suggested to account for phantom armies, one of them being that such sightings are mirages, holes in the space-time continuum, or reflections of real troops created by tricks of the light. Sir David Brewster applied this explanation to the sighting of ghostly mounted troops riding over Souter Fell in the English Lake District in June 1744. Twenty-six separate people simultaneously witnessed the event, which Brewster concluded must have been a reflection of troops on the other side of the

mountain. The flaw in his argument was that there were no troops in the vicinity at the time, but because it was shortly before the 1745 Rebellion, it is possible that secret manoeuvres had in fact been going on.

Other less mundane explanations include second sight or the result of extraterrestrial influences, but phantom armies are not always re-creations or reflections of military events. Possibly a way of explaining thunderstorms, the 'Wild Hunt' or 'Furious Host', the sighting of which is thought to presage great

BELOW: Soldiers leaving the trenches in the Battle of the Somme, during the First World War.

OPPOSITE: The Belgian town of Mons, where an angel at the head of a spectral army is said to have come to the aid of the British during the Battle of Mons in 1914.

catastrophe, such as plague or war, is a frenzied band of phantom hunters, mounted on horses and accompanied by hounds, all dashing headlong in

mad pursuit across the skies, along the ground, or just above it, to the wild accompaniment of hunting horns. There are often women among the company, and their leader is Diana, the goddess of the hunt, translated into the local female deity wherever the hunt is seen.

This is a common story in Europe, and a variation on the theme is that the hunters are fairies and spirits, led by a horned being, the person they are hunting often being a woman or a moss maiden (tree or woodland spirit). Anyone unfortunate enough to see them might either be kidnapped, taken to the land of the dead, or wither away or be sent insane, which is very different from the Victorian image of fairies, skipping through their woodland glades.

One of the most celebrated instances of a more recent phantom army includes the Angel of Mons, and all the other visions that are said to have accompanied the British retreat from the Belgian town of Mons in August 1914. Despite facing an overwhelming German force, the British were able to fall back in good order and secure their defences. Harold Begbie claimed to have obtained accounts from many soldiers present at the time, who described a wide range of visions, all rallying to the British cause. Some said ghostly knights and bowmen helped them slow the German advance, and an officer reported being aware of spectral lines of cavalry riding alongside him and his men. Others spoke of angels, complete armies in the sky, or strange clouds that hid them from the enemy.

The famous Angel of Mons is said to have appeared dressed all in white, mounted on a white charger and brandishing a flaming sword. He or she was able to rally the British troops, enabling them to halt the German advance and secure victory in the end.

Begbie wrote these accounts up as a book in response to Arthur Machen's short story about phantom Medieval bowmen helping out soldiers in the trenches. Machen maintained it was his work of fiction that had inspired this talk of visions, but Begbie riposted that it was the other way round. There never was a conclusive end to this argument.

STRANGE & SHOCKING

Friendly Fire

Spontaneous Human Combustion

Weeping Statues

Levitation

Peculiar Powers

Stigmatics

The Incorruptibles

Near-Death Experiences

Feral Children

Sky Burial

CHAPTER SIX
STRANGE & SHOCKING

FRIENDLY FIRE

We learn, from an early age, that touching hot things hurts us, which is how we survive infancy without serious injury. Yet the human body has been known to withstand deliberate exposure to fire and extreme heat, yet come out of the experience completely unscathed.

Fire-walking is certainly the best known of these phenomena, and walking barefoot across hot coals or stones is now so widespread in the West as to feature in personal development courses or as an ultimate form of sponsored walk. But the notion of ordeal by fire is rather more ancient, having been the means by which guilt or innocence was determined by giving a person a painful task to perform.

RIGHT: Used by sadhus and fakirs as a spiritual exercise, entertainers also perform feats of fire-eating using skill, trickery, and by learning to tolerate pain.

OPPOSITE: A fire-walker at Mount Lavinia in Sri Lanka.

Fire was used because of its purifying properties, and the idea was that the deity would help the innocent by performing a miracle on their behalf. Until comparatively recently, Hindus walked over red-hot iron, thus proving their innocence by escaping unharmed. Others were merely demonstrating their miraculous insensibility to fire, but there have always been exceptions, and some fire-walkers have been badly burned, perhaps as a result of guilt, lack of faith, loss of concentration, or simply by not walking fast enough.

Fire-walking developed independently in a great many cultures and over many centuries. Muslims and Hindus in India, Sri Lanka and Fuji, Navajo Native Americans, and followers of the Shinto religion in Japan have for various reasons all been practitioners, so it was only a matter of time before Europeans should have wanted to try out fire-walking for themselves.

To convince the sceptics, a scientifically conducted fire-walk was held at Carshalton, Surrey, in September 1935. Academics from the University of London witnessed Kuda Bux, an Indian Muslim, walk four times across a 20-ft (6-m) trench of

burning wood without ill-effect. One of the onlookers was not convinced, however, but when invited to try it out for himself, hastily declined.

More spectacular had been the fire-walk observed by the Catholic bishop of Mysore, near Madras, in 1921. As is so often the case, someone already proficient at the technique was present, who claimed to be capable of conferring this ability to others. He was able to persuade a local brass band, all of them Christians, to march across hot coals, which they did twice, continuing to play their instruments and emerging completely unscorched by the fire.

E.G. Stephenson, a professor of English literature, was faced with a 90-ft (27-m) charcoal trench at a Shinto ceremony in Tokyo, after a priest had taken him to a nearby temple and sprinkled salt on his head. Stephenson later wrote, in the *Journal of Borderland Research*, that all he had felt, as he made his way across the coals, was a tingling in his feet; he had been aware of one isolated sharp pain, which was found to have been caused by a cut made by a sharp stone.

So how is it done? In some cases the fire-walking is performed in a trance or a state of religious ecstasy,

while for others rituals, chanting or dancing are preliminaries to the event. There are those, however, who make no preparation at all, except perhaps to develop their own powers of concentration. But all this doesn't make fire-walkers permanently impervious; testing their feet with a pin and a lit cigarette, Dr. Harry Wright found that the feet of walkers in Fiji were sensitive to pain both immediately before and after a walk.

But fire-walking is only one aspect of this phenomenon, and a few individuals have been capable of far more spectacular feats. In the 1870s, in Maryland, USA, Nathan Coker, a blacksmith, was able to stand on a white-hot shovel in his bare feet until it cooled; he then rolled molten lead shot around his mouth until it solidified, and held glowing coals and red-hot irons in his hands, all without suffering burns. This was verified by independent witnesses, and it seems that throughout history there have been similar cases, such as people who have survived burning at the stake. In 17th-century Europe, a man named Richardson put this strange talent to good use by making a living out of it as an entertainer, one of his specialities being the eating of brimstone and molten glass, while another person was able to grip a red-hot iron bar, using his teeth to bend it into different shapes. What all of these examples indicate is that the mind having power over the body is not as fanciful as it seems, but a very powerful force indeed.

SPONTANEOUS HUMAN COMBUSTION

'She saw the corpse on the floor in the most dreadful condition. At the distance of four feet from the bed there was a heap of ashes. Her legs, with the stockings on, remained untouched, and the head, half-burned, lay between them. Nearly all the rest of the body was reduced to ashes. The air in the room was charged with floating soot. A small oil lamp on the floor was covered with ashes, but had no oil in it; and in two candlesticks, which stood upright upon a table, the cotton wick of both the candles was left, and the tallow of both had disappeared.'

Spontaneous human combustion is one of the oddest of the phenomena to affect humankind. As the above account from 1763 shows, it isn't new; it is no respecter of class and can happen to anyone, be they a tramp, a

labourer or the Contessa Cornelia di Bandi. It was described widely in 19th-century fiction, in the stories of Dickens, Zola, Melville and de Quincey, yet the phenomenon has always been real enough.

But these are not 'normal' fires. In well-documented cases it is said that the heat generated was intense enough to crack mirrors, melt bakelite switchplates and, most tellingly of all, reduce human bones to a pile of ash. In crematoria, temperatures of 2500° F are used, but even higher temperatures

are needed to incinerate bone to this extent. Yet despite such temperatures, spontaneous human combustion does not appear to cause serious damage to surroundings. All cases seem to happen in buildings, and one might have expected such intense heat to have started a major fire, yet apart from localized damage, extending a few feet

An old soldier, who died in a hayloft in Aberdeen, Scotland, possibly as a result of spontaneous human combustion. From the British Medical Journal, 21 April 1888.

The ash and remains of a woman, aged 69, who was found dead of 'preternatural combustability' in London, on 29 January 1958. Because of the position of the body she may simply have fallen into the fireplace while combustion was taking place. An ordinary domestic fire would not have been hot enough to reduce a human body to ash, and nothing else around the body has been burned or scorched.

around the body, this does not happen, and sometimes even the victim's clothes remain intact.

A typical case is that of Mary Reeser of St. Petersburg, Florida. On the morning of 1 July 1951 her landlady attempted to deliver a telegram, but found the doorknob of Mrs. Reeser's apartment too hot to touch. Two workmen managed to open the door, to be greeted by a blast of hot air, a little smoke, and a small flame burning on a partition wall. Firemen were called, easily extinguishing the flame, who then proceeded to break down the wall to find the remains of the unfortunate woman.

All that remained of Mrs. Reeser, who had been sitting in her armchair, was about 9lb (4kg) of ash, the coil springs of the armchair, and the metal framework of a nearby standard lamp, plus one of the woman's feet, still encased in a black slipper. A small piece of her backbone was still recognizable as such, but her skull had been shrunk to the size of an orange. The wall behind the armchair was unharmed, and a pile of newspapers, only a foot away, had been left unsinged. In this, one of the best documented cases of spontaneous human combustion, which was investigated by pathologists, firemen, experts on arson and insurance assessors, none could find an explanation.

How was it that Mrs. Reeser, and the many other similar victims of the phenomenon, came to die in this way? Eighteenth-century writers tended to put ithe reason fpr ot down to excessive drinking, while others were of the opinion that methane had been the cause. This inflammable gas is produced in the human gut, but has to be ignited by an external source. Diophosphane is known to spontaneously ignite, but has so far only been found in microscopic amounts in human beings, and if sufficient might possibly ignite, setting alight the methane and phosphane content in the body.

There seems to be evidence that the combustion starts from within the abdomen, burning from the inside out. In September 1967, firemen were called to a deserted building in Lambeth, London, to find a tramp lying on the stairs. His body was on fire, and an experienced officer, Jack Stacey, later told John Heymer, an ex-CID investigator, what they had seen. 'There was a four-inch slit in his abdomen from which was issuing, at force, a blue flame, which was beginning to burn the stairs. We extinguished the flames by playing a hose into the abdominal cavity. Bailey was alive when he began burning and must have been in terrible pain. His teeth were sunk into the mahogany newel post of the staircase.' This echoes the case of a sheep combusting in Dorset, England, during the Second World War. An army patrol reported that 'from its stomach issued blue flames'. As in the case of Bailey, the rest of the sheep was otherwise unharmed, the fire appearing to have started in the stomach.

The British TV programme, *QED*, with the help of Dr. John De Haan, a forensic specialist at the California Criminalistics Institute, tried to replicate spontaneous combustion by

LEFT & OPPOSITE: Mrs. Mary Reeser, who died at home in 1951. All that was left of her was her shrunken skull and one leg.

wrapping a dead pig in a blanket and placing it in a room. A small amount of petrol was lit on the pig's shoulder and the researchers withdrew. Five hours later, it was still alight, so the fire was doused, but the effects were certainly similar to human cases of the phenomenon. The pig's extremities were intact (human feet are often untouched by SHC) but its bones crumbled when poked; there was only localized heat damage in the room; and the fire had clearly been long and slow-burning, yet had produced heat extreme enough to destroy bone.

To date, modern science has been unable to deliver a complete explanation for SHC and it remains a mystery to this day.

WEEPING STATUES

Statues weeping tears of a substance which appears to be human blood, oil, or a scented liquid have all been reported, and it is a phenomenon very similar to that of the much rarer weeping paintings. Other phenomena are sometimes associated with weeping

LEFT: This statue of the Blessed Virgin Mary (Rosa Mystica) apparently shed tears of blood in September 1982.

RIGHT: In a chapel in Brooklyn, New York, on Friday, 18 May 1984, this Rosa Mystica statue wept, often copiously and for weeks afterwards. Like the other Rosa Mystica that wept in Chicago in June of the same year, this statue came from Montichiari, Italy, where the original of the type originated some years ago. To the photographer of this statue, the tears tasted salty and slightly sweet, and his efforts to wipe them away only resulted in new tears welling up in the eyes.

statues, such as miraculous healing, figures forming in the tear lines, and the scent of roses being present, effects which are in general witnessed by Christians, though not exclusively so. Weeping statues are almost always of the Virgin Mary (Rosa Mystica).

Many accept these as legitimate occurrences, despite being contrary to all natural laws, describing them as spiritual events, in that they are a form of revelation or a holy apparition.

The Catholic Church is very careful in its approach to miraculous events, for to validate a forgery would be detrimental to the church's standing in the world, while renouncing what is revered by many would be to cause great offence. This is particularly true of weeping statues, due to the inexplicability of the phenomenon.

To claim that a statue weeps is dismissed by some as pure imagination, the witnesses being either deluded or in the grip of mass religious fervour causing an altered state of mind. If this were the case, however, the phenomenon could not have been captured on video, as has been the case in many instances, neither could some statues have been tested and found to have been weeping real human tears or blood.

Another possible explanation is that the so-called tears can be attributed to condensation, the beads of moisture coming from microscopic cracks in the statues' porous fabric. Unpublished reports of these having been tested have

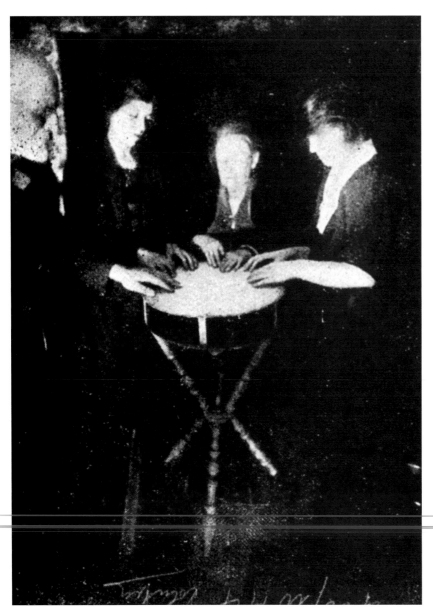

supposedly been able to verify this theory, but true scientific research into the phenomenon has rarely, if ever, been carried out, while some examples have been dismissed as hoaxes.

LEVITATION

'I feel no hands supporting me, and, since the first time, I have never felt fear; though, should I have fallen from the ceiling of some rooms in which I have been raised, I could not have escaped serious injury. I am generally lifted up perpendicularly; my arms frequently become rigid, and are drawn above my head, as if I were grasping the unseen power which slowly raises me from the floor.'

LEFT: A séance in which a table is seen to be levitating.

OPPOSITE: Indian magician Yusultini and his wife and partner, Faeeza, perform their levitation act on a beach near Durban, South Africa. Yusultini took up the challenge to perform levitation in the open air to disprove the theory that he made use of thin wires. The picture is not a fake, but when asked if there was a trick involved he answered 'certainly', but would not disclose what it was.

So wrote Daniel Douglas Home, a 19th-century medium who discovered he had the power to levitate at will. There is no doubt that many of the claimed cases of human levitation are based on self-deception, or plain and simple fraud. But there are a few, accompanied by well-documented accounts from impeccable sources, that are simply impossible to dismiss. There is little doubt that some people have sufficient control over their own bodies to defy gravity, allowing them to rise into the air, and some presumably can accomplish this at will.

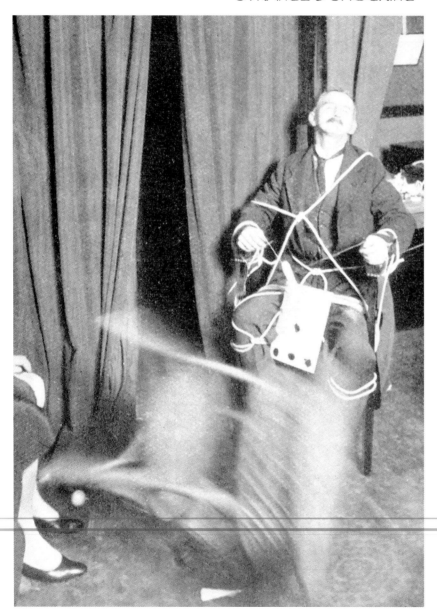

Daniel Home was 19 when he discovered this peculiar ability. He was already a famous medium, and was at the centre of a séance in Connecticut in the summer of 1852 when levitation occurred. The man seated next to him in the hand-holding circle was F.L. Burr, the editor of the *Hereford Times*, and this is what he had to say: 'Suddenly, without any expectation on the part of the company, Home was taken up in the air. I had hold of his hand at the time and I felt his feet – they were lifted a foot from the floor. He palpitated from head to foot with the contending emotions of joy and fear, which choked his utterances. Again and again he was taken from the floor, and the third time he was carried to the ceiling of the apartment, with which his hands and feet came into gentle contact.'

LEFT: Here a table is levitating so rapidly as to be a blur in the photograph. Note that the medium, J. Lewis, is in a catatonic trance, working under test conditions at the College of Psychic Science, London, in May 1928.

OPPOSITE: A table levitating during a séance in Milan in 1892, conducted by the Italian medium, Eusapia Palladino.

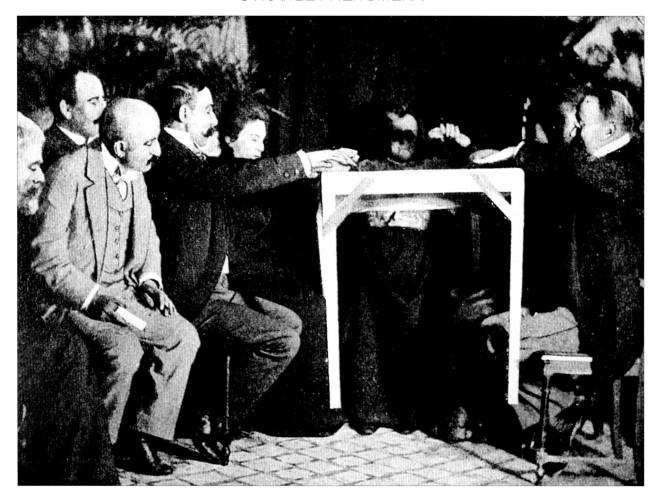

This first levitation took Daniel Home, as well as everyone around him, completely by surprise, and he later learned to perform the feat at will, making 'flights' in front of many witnesses, including Mark Twain, John Ruskin, W.M. Thackeray and even the Emperor Napoleon III of France. For 40 years or so, Home levitated before amazed audiences, although not all of them were uncritical. One of Home's most famous performances was in July 1871 at the London apartment of Lord Adare, in the presence of several eminent observers. He was seen to float out of one window of the apartment and in at another. Those present believed what they had seen, but a

Jesuit scholar, Father Herbert
Thurston, who had spent a lifetime
studying the phenomenon of levitating
objects and people, gave a convincing
explanation as to how Home had been
able to deceive his witnesses.

If Daniel Home was a fraud, then
he must have fooled a great many

*ABOVE: India: a boy, presumably
suspended in mid-air supported by a stick.*

*RIGHT: Here, Father Quevedo has been
able to induce a girl to levitate.*

Demonstrating the levitation of a pair of scissors, in the same manner as Polish medium, Stanislawa Tomczyk, performed the feat in the first decade of the 20th century.

people, and William Crookes, one of Victorian Britain's most eminent scientists, was obviously one of them. After witnessing the events at Lord Adare's apartment Crookes wrote: 'The phenomena I am prepared to attest are so extraordinary, and so directly oppose the most firmly-rooted articles of scientific belief – amongst others, the ubiquity and invariable action of the force of gravitation – that, even now, on recalling the details of what I

witnessed, there is an antagonism in my mind between reason, which pronounces it to be scientifically impossible, and the consciousness that my senses, both of touch and light, are not lying witnesses.'

Critics would say that Crookes and his contemporaries simply fell victim to the type of mass hypnosis that prevails in the Indian rope trick, in which a different reality is experienced (the boy assistant disappearing at the top of the magically erect rope) to the actual reality (magician and assistant are standing impassively by the rope, which is coiled on the ground). Photographic evidence, however, shows that it only a trick after all. Does any convincing photographic evidence of levitation actually exist?

Pictures can be faked, but the set taken by P.T. Plunkett in southern India in 1936 are strangely convincing. Plunkett arranged to watch the fakir, Subbyaha Pullavar, at 12.30pm, when the sun was overhead, so that no

Joey A. Nuzum, of Washington, Pennsylvania, has paranormal mental and physical abilities, as attested by Dr. B.E. Schwarz, who has studied him for years. Here we see Joey levitating.

trickery would be concealed by shadows. The actual levitation took place inside a tent, hidden from view, which was removed once the fakir was a few feet off the ground; Plunkett was then permitted to take pictures from all angles.

The fakir's hand was resting lightly on a stick, though clearly it was to help his balance rather than keep him in the air. When the time came to descend, the tent was again erected around the fakir, though Plunkett maintained that the tent's fabric was so thin as to allow him clearly to see the man gently descend to the ground in the same prone position, with no attempt made at stealthily removing himself from some hidden support.

Was this merely a clever confidence trick, or was it simply the result of self-control and the ability to focus strongly on the matter in hand?

PECULIAR POWERS

We all remember the physics class at school, when generating static electricity made a classmate's hair stand on end, or even produced a small electric shock. For most of us, that is as far as it goes, but a few individuals appear to harbour, within their

bodies, extraordinary electrical power, or magnetism, the question being whether this a biological or a paranormal phenomenon.

Several such cases were reported throughout the 19th century, and those involved were often adolescent girls, whose powers appear to have been involuntary. Angélique Cottin, from La Perrière in France, was 14 when she discovered the unsettling effect she had on inanimate objects. Pieces of heavy furniture would jump up and down, or spin away from her when she touched them lightly, and physicist François Arago noted that compasses went haywire when she was in the vicinity. He also found the effect to be stronger in the evening and that it seemed to emanate from her left side, leading him to conclude that it was akin to electromagnetism. Angélique's power lasted for only ten weeks, which was just as well; her heart had been racing at 120 beats per minute while all this was going on and she had been made terrified by the whole experience.

Frank McKinstry of Joplin, Missouri, was the subject of a study in 1889, in that he was obliged to keep moving to prevent his feet from becoming stuck to the ground, and that

when the phenomenon came upon him, passersby would have to come to his aid to prise them free. The magnetism of others is shown just as graphically. Sixteen-year-old Louis Hamburger was examined by the Maryland College of Pharmacy in 1890. Louis could lift a glass jar full of iron filings, weighing about 5lb (2.25kg), using only the tips of three fingers. He could also make metal objects stick to his skin, as could Caroline Clare from Ontario.

In fact, the late-19th century seems to have seen a spate of such cases in the United States, and young Lulu Hurst of Georgia actually made a brief stage career using her unusual powers. These began when strange rapping noises were heard in her bedroom, which answered yes or no to questions, much like spirits at a séance. But it was her sudden superhuman strength that startled her most. She would lightly touch a chair while five men tried to move it, or lift three men seated on the same chair by resting her open palms on its back. Researchers were allowed to examine Lulu closely, but could find no evidence of fraud.

The Universal Council for Psychic Research could be described as sceptical to a fault. In 1938 it met in New York,

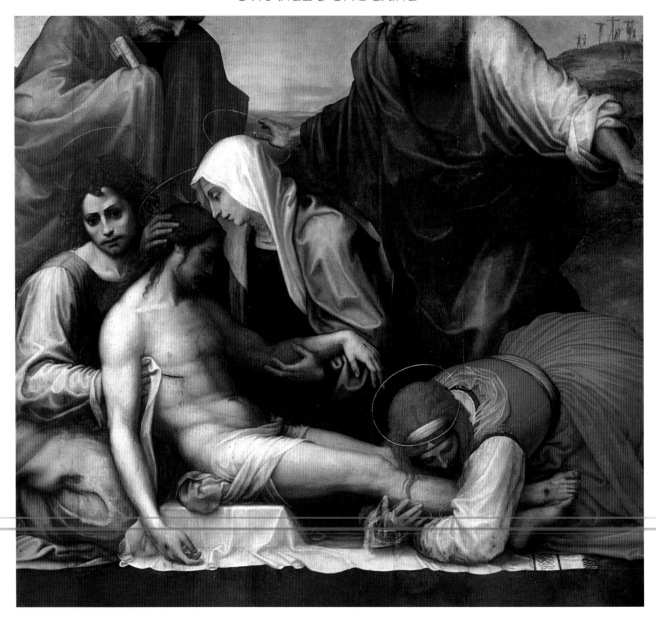

The Descent from the Cross (Deposition), a painting by Fra Bartolommeo (1472–1517) in the Pitti Palace, Florence, Italy. Here the dead Christ has been taken down from the Cross and is being tended by His Mother. The painting shows the wounds of His Passion known, when they appear in others, as the stigmata.

offering a prize of $10,000 for demonstrations of psychic powers. Proving that human magnetism was not the monopoly of the young, an elderly lady, Antoine Timmer, presented herself and showed how cutlery stuck to her hands as if they were magnets. But she didn't get her $10,000: Joseph Dunninger, the chairman of the council and himself an illusionist, dismissed her with the claim that he could do the same by means of hidden threads. This was perhaps missing the point, which had been to test whether or not Mrs. Timmer had genuine powers, and if so, to discover the reason for them.

Science may not have been able to explain these extreme forms of human magnetism, but authors Bob Rickard and Jon Michell (*The Rough Guide to Unexplained Phenomena*) thought it was a sort of poltergeist effect. Flying furniture and odd powers are associated

with the paranormal, from which conventional science sometimes shies away. That same science does accept that bio-electrics exist, however, present most spectacularly in the case of the electric eel. In the 1930s, even Professor Harold Saxton-Burr, of Yale University, knew that all living creatures probably generate their own magnetic fields, but that they are usually fairly weak. It was a case that Lulu and her friends simply had powers on a very different scale.

Human electrical activity is often associated with illness or recovery: in 1920, 34 inmates of Clinton Prison, New York, went down with botulinus poisoning, and all were afflicted by excess static electricity, affecting compasses and metal objects, effects which diminished as the men recovered. In 1976 12-year-old Vyvyan Jones, of Bristol, England, broke his arm. For two days his hair stood on end and he was found to be producing enough static electricity to illuminate light bulbs when holding them in his hands. There might also be a connection with grief or emotional shock: in the early 1970s, Dr. Leonard J. Ravitz submitted a colleague to hypnotic regression to recall a moment of grief, measuring a 14-millivolt rise in current that lasted for

two-and-a-half minutes. Whatever the cause, human magnetism or bio-electricity seems to exist and is a very strange phenomenon indeed.

STIGMATICS

Stigmata are marks on the body which correspond to the wounds believed to have been inflicted on Jesus during His Passion and Crucifixion. Whether those affected by such wounds are truly sharing in the sufferings of Christ, or whether the phenomenon is purely psychological in origin, is an argument that is ongoing, for new stigmatics continue to appear in modern times.

The first to receive the stigmata was St. Francis of Assisi in 1224, and former BBC religious correspondent, Ted Harrison, in his 1998 book, *Stigmata*, records 406 cases that have occurred since that time. There is no doubt, therefore, that stigmata, as a phenomenon, exist; the question is, what is their cause?

What is clear is that the recipients are overwhelmingly female (87 per cent, according to Harrison's list), but only two out of three are members of an established religion. Given the overtly religious connotations attached to the stigmata (or, to be more accurate, what

Cross. Thomas de Celano, writing not long after Francis's death, described them as 'the prints of the nails, but the nails themselves formed out of his flesh and retaining the blackness of the iron', while another writer, St. Bonaventure, described them as projecting through the soles of the feet and clenched over, but so large that it was difficult to place the soles of the feet flat on the ground.

A later stigmatic, who became the subject of scientific study, was Domenica Lazzari, who also had these 'nails' in her feet, though not to the same degree as St. Francis. Dr. Dei Cloche studied Domenica, writing up the results in 1837. It seems that after suffering what could be described as a traumatic shock, the girl developed a serious case of hyperesthesia. This is a recognized medical condition, in which the patient becomes extraordinarily sensitive to touch and temperature, or indeed anything that can be

are largely perceived to be such) this is in itself something of a surprise.

St. Francis, as well as being the first recorded stigmatic, appears to have had the most dramatic manifestations of Christ's wounds. The stigmata usually consist of wounds on the hands, feet, forehead or side which, on occasion, bleed copiously. The marks on Francis's hands and feet actually appeared to reproduce the very means by which Christ was nailed to the

ABOVE: El Greco's painting of St. Francis of Assisi.

RIGHT: Domenica Lazzari's stigmata was so severe as to cause her to be bed-ridden for 11 years until her death in 1848.

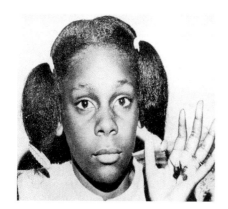

experienced by the five senses. In Domenica's case she was deafened by normal noise and dazzled by even moderate light.

She was also in constant pain and later developed wounds on her hands and side, with a row of puncture marks around her forehead that could be interpreted as caused by a crown of

ABOVE: Cloretta Robertson, aged 9, of Oakland, California, displayed stigmata which appeared a few weeks before Good Friday 1972, when they disappeared.

RIGHT: Antonio Ruffini saw an apparition of the Virgin Mary and received the stigmata in 1951, the wounds penetrating his hands and feet. He built a chapel on the site of his vision south of Rome. This photograph was taken in 1987.

thorns. On the back of each hand was a black, domed lump, like the head of a nail, and in the palms, deep incisions which bled freely. Lord Shrewsbury also examined her, noting that, 'Instead of taking its normal course, the blood flowed downwards over the toes, as it would do were she suspended on a cross'. Her forehead wounds bled too, which happened every Friday, the day of the week on which Jesus was crucified. But the blood, according to Lord Shrewsbury, seemed to disappear 'of itself'. Domenica lived bedridden with her stigmata for 11 years and no

evidence of trickery was ever discovered. Interestingly, she was neither excessively religious nor was she obsessed with the Crucifixion. She died in 1848.

Domenica's stigmata had been long-lived, but that of Cloretta Robertson lasted for a much shorter time. Nineteen days before Easter 1972, bloody marks appeared on her hands which were in evidence for a few minutes each day. The stigmata ceased on Good Friday that same year and never reappeared. Cloretta was also the first black, non-Catholic stigmatic on

LEFT: *Theresa Neumann displaying her stigmata scars.*

BELOW: *Theresa Neumann, shown bleeding profusely from her stigmata.*

OPPOSITE LEFT: *The Italian stigmatic Giorgio Bongiovanni, photographed in 1993, who received his stigmata during a visit to Fatima. The five wounds bleed almost daily.*

OPPOSITE RIGHT: *John Snide, who in 1998 received the stigmata and apparitions of the Virgin Mary.*

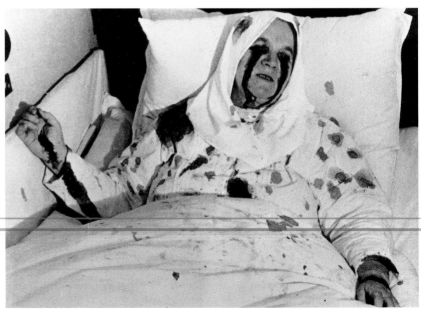

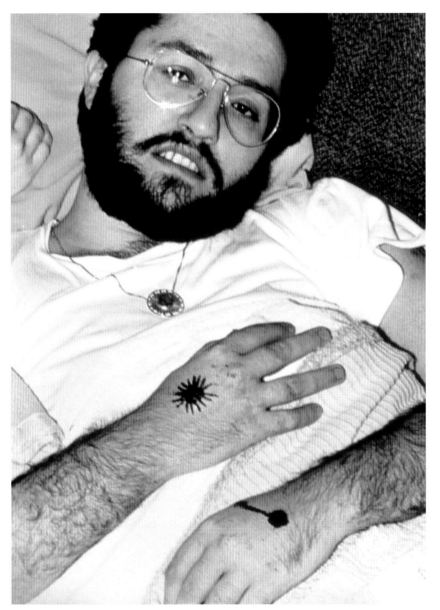

record. Her marks may have been slight, but contrast them with those of Theresa Neumann, who died ten years earlier. She bled every Friday, but in her case would lose nearly a pint of blood each time, from her hands, feet, sides and forehead, not to mention 8lb (4kg) in weight.

There is scientific evidence that stigmata are psychogenic in origin – that is, physical effects that originate in the mind or come out of mental or emotional conflict, and Ted Harrison certainly found evidence of trauma in the previous lives of his stigmatics.

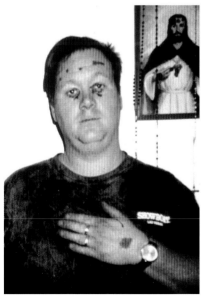

LEFT: In 1998 John Snide (see page 159)
experienced several religious phenomena, including bleeding images of Christ.

OPPOSITE: The body of St. Catherine Labouré, whose visions of the Virgin Mary in 1830 led her to create the Miraculous Medal worn by millions of Catholics today. Despite her death in 1876, her body, when it was exhumed, was seen to have suffered no deterioration.

Looking at six modern cases, he found that some had been subjected to sexual molestation, or physical abuse that was sometimes self-inflicted, while others suffered from Munchausen's Syndrome (the feigning of disease to gain attention), having 'extremely low self-esteem bordering on self-hatred'.

Rickard and Michell point out that the same characteristics are often true of people claiming to have been abducted by aliens. The Italian stigmatic, Georgio Bongiovanni, currently still living, claims to have visions of Jesus and Mary descending from a UFO. But the evidence for the psychological origin of stigmata is powerful, and the effects have been reproduced, albeit in a less intense form, under hypnosis.

THE INCORRUPTIBLES
The causes of incorruptibility are disputed, but the two main positions can be summarized either as an argument for a spiritual or supernatural cause or an argument for one that is physical or environmental. That for a spiritual cause may include a belief that the inherent sanctity of an individual may in some way have imbued their flesh with something that prevents decomposition after death, or that it was caused by the intervention of the deity.

Many specimens of preserved human bodies, or 'mummies', have been discovered, some dating from before Pharaonic times in Egypt, where the art of embalming reached its apogee. Many of these have survived decomposition for 3,000 years or more, but of the many types discovered over the centuries, some of the bodies were in fact accidentally preserved, having been buried in dry, hot sand or in an area where there was high radioactivity. These bodies were able to escape significant but not total decay as long as air or moisture did not reach them.

This statue in the Cathedral of Ste.-Cécile at Albi, in the French Pyrenees, is a copy of The Martyrdom of St. Cecilia *by Stefano Maderno. There was an attempt to kill her by suffocating her in an overheated bath house, which she survived, then three attempts at beheading her failed. She later died of her wounds and was buried as she died. Her grave was discovered in 817, and her body was removed to the church now known as Santa Cecilia in Trastevere, Rome. The tomb was opened in 1599, when her uncorrupted body was revealed. She is one of the earliest of the incorruptibles to have been exhumed.*

Such bodies are typically discoloured, wrinkled, distorted and inflexible, and are permeated with the smell of death. Once disturbed they quickly fall into a state of decay.

There are other corpses, however, that have been deliberately embalmed or otherwise treated before burial, with the intention of preventing or slowing down decay. As long as the bodies are sealed against air and moisture they can be significantly but not totally preserved. The ancient Egyptians achieved this by removing the body organs and filling the cavities with natron before tightly bandaging the

body and packing it in more of the salt. In more modern methods of preservation a variety of preservatives, sanitizers, disinfectant agents and additives are used to temporarily delay decomposition and restore a natural appearance for viewing a body after death. Again, when disturbed, the bodies are found to be in a similar state as the accidentally preserved, and are similarly malodorous.

But there is another type of incorruptible that seems to have defied decay due to extraordinary forces lying in the realms of the supernatural. Bodies such as these began to be discovered soon after the death of Christ, and the fact that they had escaped the decay of death has baffled scientists for centuries. While the phenomenon is mainly connected with Christianity, similar examples of incorruptibility have been claimed in other cultures.

According to the Roman Catholic Church, a body cannot be deemed incorruptible if it has undergone an embalming process or other means of preservation. The body should remain completely flexible, as if it is only sleeping, and despite the length of time it has lain in the tomb, sometimes for

centuries, is typically imbued with a sweet smell that many describe as rose-scented. Other partial incorruptibles have been found throughout the centuries where certain parts of the body have decayed normally, while other parts, such as the heart or tongue, have remained in perfect condition.

In Catholic and Orthodox Christian cultures, incorruptibility is generally regarded as a sign that the individual is a saint, although not every saint is expected to be an incorruptible. What is astonishing is that nearly all incorruptibles were, in life, extremely devout Christians, which would point to the fact that a miracle of sorts has occurred. Nearly all of such bodies have been identified and their backgrounds thoroughly researched. Many have been canonized as saints, their incorruptibility regarded as evidence of their extreme sanctity and devotion to God when they lived in this world.

NEAR-DEATH EXPERIENCES

One day, during the reign of Queen Victoria, Stainton Moses was travelling peacefully down the River Isis in Oxford on a boating trip, when he collided with another boat and was almost drowned. This is how he

described the experience: 'As I could not swim a stroke, I soon sank…I floundered about until, I suppose, I became unconscious. At any rate, a strange peacefulness took the place of my previous feeling. I recognized fully that I was drowning, but no sort of fear was present to my mind. I did not even regret the fact. By degrees, as it seemed – though the process must have been instantaneous – I recollected my life…The next thing I remember was the interruption of this peaceful state by a series of most unpleasant sensations which were attendant on resuscitation.'

Stainton Moses's experience is far from unique, and there are many documented cases of what have come to be known as near-death experiences. What happens to human consciousness after death remains one of life's big questions. Established religions claim the soul proceeds to heaven, hell, or is reborn into another physical life. Whether or not one subscribes to this theory, there are plenty of such first-hand experiences on record, which share many common features. Perhaps the most persistent is the well-known sensation of one's whole life 'flashing before one's eyes'. According to those who have experienced it, every detail, both good and bad, is seen simultaneously, in what has been described as a 'life review' or even a 'personal judgement day', in a blink-of-an-eye summation of an entire life.

Geologist S.W. Cozzens experienced such a flash of consciousness when he fell off a mountain in Arizona, leading him to write about his experience in his book, *The Marvellous Country*, in 1875. 'Convinced that death was inevitable, I became perfectly reconciled to the thought. My mind comprehended in a moment the acts of a lifetime. Transactions of the most trivial character…the remembrance of which had been buried deep in memory's vault for years, stood before me in bold relief; my mind recalled with the rapidity of lightning and yet retained a distinct impression of thought. I seemed to be gliding swiftly and surely out of the world, but felt no fear, experienced no regret at the prospect.' Cozzens' reference to a feeling of peace and lack of regret echoes the experience of Stainton Moses, and is in fact a recurring theme of most near-death experiences. The individual is absolutely clear that death is imminent, and is not only resigned to the fact but also appears almost to welcome it.

Such accounts are also referred to as 'out-of-body experiences'; modern psychiatrists Russell Noyes and Ray Kletti interviewed many people who had had them, all of whom narrowly escaped death. Fifty-seven had survived serious falls, 54 car crashes, 48 drownings, 27 miscellaneous near-fatal accidents, and 29 serious illnesseses. Interestingly, the proportion reporting life reviews varied according to the nature of the incident. Almost half of the near-drowned had this experience, but of those who fell only 16 per cent reported the fact. Other medical studies show a huge variation in the number of people who, having had such an experience, have presumably cheated death, which was between 2 and 47 per cent.

Another aspect of the experience often produces a sensation of 'floating' outside the body, in which the person clearly remembers looking back and seeing their own body from a distance, as if in some way their consciousness had left it. An example of this is that of the patient undergoing a serious operation, who has the sensation of floating above the operating table, watching their own body on which the procedure is being carried out.

This floating sensation is sometimes associated with travelling to a new place, either through a tunnel towards a great light, or crossing a river or proceeding down a long corridor. At the other end, a familiar figure – either religious, a friend or family member – is there to greet the traveller. Dr. Robert Crookall found that these details often vary between cultures, which would suggest they are based on folk-memories or religious beliefs.

Of course, there are many who are sceptical of any sort of spiritual dimension being attached to the experience. Dr. Susan Blackmore, in her book, *Dying to Live*, attributes these sensations to oxygen starvation and neural hallucinations emanating from the optic nerve. As for the feelings of peace and well-being, these she puts down to a flood of endorphins in the temporal lobe.

Whatever the explanation, there is no doubt that near-death experiences are very real to those who have experienced them, and survivors see the world in a very different light thereafter, becoming determined to live a full life, perhaps even a better one, as a result.

FERAL CHILDREN

Romulus, according to tradition the founder of Rome, and his brother Remus, the twin sons of Mars and Rhea Silvia, were left at birth by the River Tiber, but were found by a she-wolf who suckled them, and they were eventually brought up by shepherds. Rudyard Kipling's Mowgli is another wolf-boy, and although these examples may not actually be true, there are plenty of accounts of children who

BELOW: Feral children: a boy takes biscuits from a woman's hand.

RIGHT: The famous statue of Romulus and Remus being suckled by a she-wolf. Romulus grew up to become the founder of Rome.

really have been reared by animals from a young age. Of those who have been rescued and returned to human society it has been observed that feral children, recaptured when they are still young, seem unable to relate with people and invariably long to return to their old life in the wild.

It has long been maintained by some that these are not normal, healthy children who happen to have been brought up by non-human animals, but children who have been severely neglected by their human parents, hence their inability to learn or adopt human habits. This is also characterized by an inability to speak, a liking for raw food, and a desire to run around naked.

French anthropologist, Jean-Claude Armen, who discovered a boy living as part of a gazelle herd in the Sahara Desert, took the opposite view that while damaged children would be unable to adapt to life in the wild, feral children who had never enjoyed human contact clearly could. Perhaps the

LEFT: Two feral children, allegedly raised by wolves, lay asleep.

OPPOSITE: A feral boy reared by wolves and found in India in February 1954.

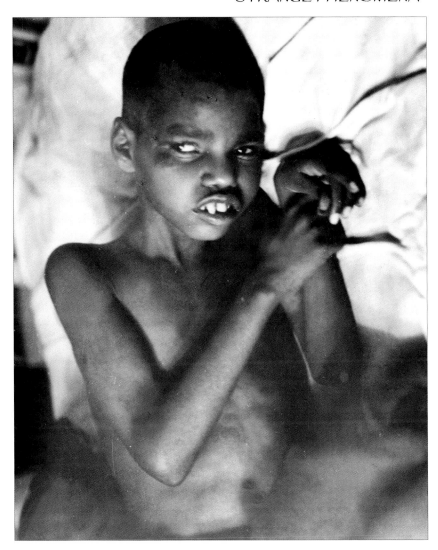

There are stories of children being raised by all sorts of animals, wolves being the most common, but there are also accounts of monkeys, bears, cattle, pigs, sheep, gazelle, big cats (panthers and leopards), goats and even ostriches assuming a motherly role. R.M. Zingg, of Denver University, made a study of 32 recorded cases of feral children up to 1940. Their ages ranged from 18 months to 23 years and all but five were boys or young men. Where the animal involved was known, most turned out to be wolves, and over half the children walked on all fours; only a minority were successfully taught to walk on two legs by their human captors. The vast majority could not speak, and several made animal-like sounds and, as with walking, they were unable to learn or relearn human speech, apart from a few words. Eating habits were also clearly a result of environment. The Irish boy found in 1672, allegedly brought up by sheep, would only eat grass and hay, whereas children reared in a wolf pack relished raw meat. They usually ate on all fours, lapping up liquids like a dog.

Jean-Claude Armen treated the gazelle boy with great sensitivity,

difficulty in accepting this is the implication that there is nothing inherently 'civilized' about human beings, and that given the right environment and upbringing we would all revert to a primitive type.

winning his trust while studying him carefully. He never revealed where the boy could been found, for fear that others would come looking for him. He described him as having 'lively, dark, almond-shaped eyes and a pleasant open expression (not sullen like the children reared by carnivorous animals). He appeared to be ten years old; his ankles were disproportionately thick and obviously powerful.'

Over a few days, Armen got close to the boy by seating himself near to the herd and calmly playing his flute, without attempting to get closer. Eventually a senior gazelle came over and nuzzled him, followed by the boy. '[He] sniffs my toes, still showing a few furtive traces of fear despite his great boldness and fitfully screwing up his nose, after the manner of his adoptive mentors.' Having gained the boy's trust,

LEFT: The Wolf-Boy of Allahbad, photographed in June 1954, is India's second such boy.

OPPOSITE: Specialists and doctors crowd around the wolf-boy, Ramu, as he lies on a hospital bed ready for inspection on 18 August 1960.

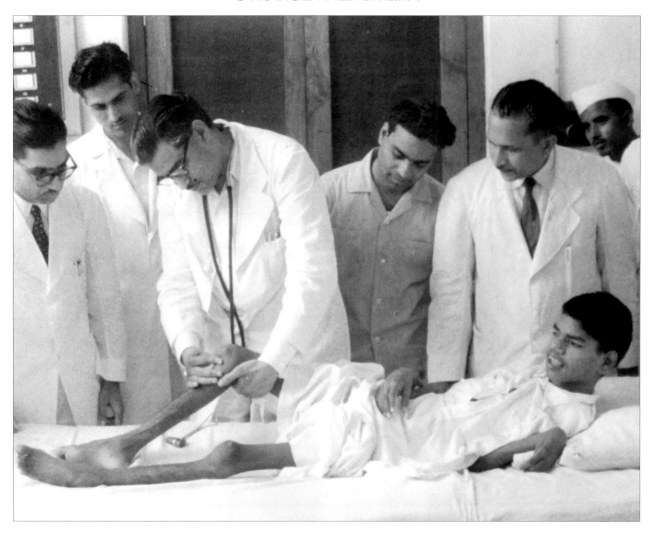

Armen was able to observe him at close quarters, concluding he had become completely integrated with the herd. He leaped and jumped about like a gazelle, with great agility, and would twitch his ears and scalp at any suspicious noise. He even adopted the sign language of the gazelles and, like them, fed on the root of the dhanoun: '...teeth first, he peels them with clicks of his tongue, then cuts them up frantically with his incisors.'

Armen wrote of his experiences, and *Gazelle Boy* was published in 1974. Another gazelle boy, with superb eyesight and acute hearing, had been reported in *The Sunday Times* the previous year, who was said to be capable of running at a speed of 50mph (80kmh). American scientists later tried to find Armen's gazelle boy, but never found him.

The reverse is true of the wolf-children of Midnapore in India. They were discovered in 1920 by the Reverend J.A.L. Singh, while he was investigating village tales of two small ghostly creatures with blazing eyes, who kept company with a female wolf. After glimpsing the 'ghosts', Singh saw that they were two 'hideous-looking' children, running about on all fours. Their lair was found in a disused antheap, and Singh had it surrounded by villagers, hoping to dig the wolves out. Two wolves fled, but a third female stood her ground, desperately trying to drive the villagers off. Before the Reverend Singh could stop them, one had shot her through with an arrow.

Inside the lair, two children were found, huddled together with two wolf cubs. They were both girls, aged about 8 and 18 months. Taken to Midnapore

orphanage, the younger child died within a year, but the elder survived another nine years, cared for by Mrs. Singh. She eventually learned to stand, to eat cooked food, and to speak a few words.

More recently, John Sseybunya of Uganda achieved a more complete reintegration into human society, though his time with animals had been relatively short. He was already 4-years-old when he escaped into the wild, claiming to have fled after witnessing the murder of his mother by his father. No one saw him for a year, but he was spotted with a group of monkeys raiding a crop. He was captured by local women, and apart from being malnourished seemed to be quite unharmed. A BBC documentary, made in 1999 when John was a young adult, revealed him to be relatively backward, but it was difficult to say whether this was inherent or because of his year spent with the monkeys. But the telling part of John's story, and evidence that it was true, was the close rapport he was able to maintain with the monkeys, communicating with them in a way that few humans ever achieve. Perhaps this is more reason to suppose that humans are affected as much by nurture as they are by nature.

Yazd, Iran. Zoroastrian Towers of Silence, on which the bodies of the dead are left to be consumed by vultures.

SKY BURIAL

There is no mystery about sky burial, and in the context of rural Tibet it makes perfect sense, however shocking it may appear to people from other cultures. Put simply, instead of corpses being buried or cremated, sky burial sees them cut into small pieces and placed on high rocks in the mountains for animals and birds of prey to dispose of in their own way.

This form of 'burial' is not unique to Tibetan culture: in Neolithic Britain bodies were often treated in this way. If the recipient was rich enough to have a special burial mound made on a hilltop, the body was left out, perhaps for months, until the weather, birds and animals had dealt with the flesh and the smaller bones. The rest of the skeleton was then buried in the mound with due reverence. This is not unlike the way the dead are treated by the Zoroastrians, a pre-Islamic religion stemming from ancient Persia and practised by Parsees today. Because the elements of earth and fire can never be

contaminated by the impurities of human flesh, burial and cremation are therefore unacceptable. Consequently, the Parsees, as in Tibet, also bury their dead in the sky, which means leaving them on high buildings, known as Towers of Silence, to be devoured by the vultures.

Tibetan sky burials vary from those of the Zoroastrians in that they have a basis in Buddhism. This teaches reincarnation, the dead body simply being an empty vessel, since the soul moves on to another life. The ritual is known in Tibet as *jhator*, which literally

A Tibetan sky burial, where vultures perform their important task.

means 'giving alms to the birds'. This is seen as an act of generosity and a fitting use for human remains, in that the dead are helping things that are still living to thrive, which is consistent with the Buddhist teaching of compassion for all forms of life, the same motive that encourages others to donate their vital organs to help others after death. Vultures in particular benefit, and as their droppings sink back into the ground the Tibetan dead can be said to be returning from whence they came.

There is a practical benefit, too. In this mountainous country the ground is often too rocky for digging graves, while fuel for cremation is scarce. Not only does this form of disposal conserve scarce resources, it returns the dead body directly to the food chain, making it perhaps the most environmentally friendly method of all. It is also thought that the process of *jhator,* in that it also involves an intimate knowledge of the human body, helps the advance of traditional Tibetan medicine.

Jhator was banned in the 1960s, but since the 1980s has been reintroduced. It is now the most common form of body disposal, though non-Tibetans are very seldom permitted to watch. It is performed on a large flat rock, higher than the surrounding area and set aside for the purpose. It usually takes place at dawn, and relatives of the dead may attend nearby, though they won't necessarily see what happens.

After the monks have chanted a mantra, they set about dismembering the body, seemingly treating it like any other rouine task, talking and laughing while they work. This is not callousness, simply a reflection of the Buddhist belief that reverence should be reserved for the departed soul or spirit rather than for the body's empty shell.

The exact process of *jhator* may vary, but according to some accounts the limbs are removed and the body hacked to pieces; the flesh and bones are then pounded together with *tsampa* (barley flour with tea and yak butter or milk), and the vultures are then free to come in and feast. Sometimes the whole body is given to the vultures intact, and it is only when the bones have been picked clean that they are ground up with *tsampa* and given to the crows and hawks. It has been observed that, at busy *jhator* sites, where there are several offerings a day, the birds have to be coaxed to come and eat, but at others, where the process is less often performed, they may have to be fended off with sticks until the body is ready.

Pamela Logan witnessed a sky burial at Drigung, Tibet, on 26 September 1997, writing of her experience for the China Exploration and Research Society. After describing the somewhat shocking spectacle, she concluded: 'Half an hour later, the body has completely disappeared. The men leave also, their day's work finished. Soon, the hilltop is restored to serenity. I think of the man whose flesh is now soaring over the mountains, and decide that, if I happen to die on the high plateau, I wouldn't mind following him.'

EXTREME NATURE

Tsunamis

Balls of Fire

The Aurora Borealis

Dust Devils & Water Spouts

Supercells, Sprites & Blue Jets

Hurricanes, Typhoons & Cyclones

CHAPTER SEVEN
EXTREME NATURE

TSUNAMIS

Until 26 December 2004, very few had ever heard of tsunamis, but by the end of the day no one was in any doubt as to the gravity of the disaster that had occurred. The Indian Ocean tsunami was the result of an earthquake which displaced vast amounts of water. This caused a series of waves which raced out from the epicentre, 100 miles (160km) off the coast of Sumatra, to hit the coasts of every land mass around the Indian Ocean. Much of that coast is densely populated and the death toll was devastating. Over 225,000 people perished in 11 countries, making this the deadliest incidence of its kind in human history. Around 1.7 million people lost their homes and thousands of others were never found. Never before has a natural catastrophe taken such a high human toll.

There have been tsunamis before, and in parts of Japan they are sufficiently common for walls to have been built, up to 15ft (4.5m) high, to protect densely populated coastal areas

from the waves. The word tsunami is derived from the Japanese *tsu* (wave) and *nami* (harbour). The wave effects can be caused by a variety of earth movements: earthquakes, volcanic explosions, landslides and even impacts from meteoroids. Of course, the effects can be very minor and barely noticeable at all.

On Boxing Day 1964 the earthquake was caused by two tectonic plates, the India and the Burma, moving towards one another. The forces involved in such movements are simply unimaginable on a human scale, and it is thought that nearly 1,000 miles (1600km) of faultline slipped about 50ft (15m) along the subduction zone, where the India plate slid under Burma. Within several minutes, a rupture 250 miles (400km) long had opened up, 19 miles (30km) beneath the seabed. It is believed that this underground movement involved a force of 9,560 gigatons of TNT, or the equivalent of 550 million Hiroshima atomic bombs, while on the surface this was translated

into 26.3 megatons of TNT or 1500 Hiroshimas. The effect on the seabed itself was devastating enough: ridges as high as 5,000ft (1500m) collapsed, causing landslides several kilometres wide and exposing a huge oceanic trench in the earthquake zone, the displaced water dragging massive slabs of rock weighing millions of tons up to 7 miles (11km) along the seabed.

But it was the rise in the seabed, by several metres, that would cause the tsunami. This displaced an estimated 7 cubic miles of water, the waves radiating out from the 1,000-mile length of the rupture. But at that point, in very deep oceanic water, the resulting waves were little more than gentle swells, though moving at the tremendous speed of over 300mph (485km/h). The waves only develop their devastating size in the shallower coastal waters, which results in an increase in the wave height in order to

The long, high, curling sea wave caused by a tsunami or other disturbance.

LEFT: Sumatra, 1 January 2005, where
Indonesian refugees wait for an
approaching helicopter bringing them food
and supplies.

OPPOSITE LEFT: Boats washed ashore
by the vast surge at Aceh, Sumatra.

felt the quake they fled to the inland
hills and thus survived. On the beach in
northern Phuket, Thailand, a ten-year-
old tourist remembered hearing about
tsunamis from school, recognized the
warning of the receding sea, and raised
the alarm. But most of the people,
stranded on the coasts when the series
of waves hit, were killed.

According to relief agencies, one-
third of the casualties were children,
partly because of the young population
in many areas, partly because they were
least likely to be able to resist the
strong currents. About 9,000 foreign
tourists, mostly European, also lost
their lives. Indonesia, Sri Lanka, India,
Thailand, the Maldives, Somalia,
Burma, Malaysia and the Seychelles
were all badly affected, with states of
emergency being declared in many
areas. As well as the immediate need to
rescue survivors, there were fears that
diseases, such as cholera and typhoid,

conserve their total energy. The waves
slowed right down to tens of miles per
hour, transferring their energy into
height, so that by the time they hit the
coast they were up to 80ft (24m) tall.
The coast closest to the epicentre was
hit just 15 minutes after the earthquake
occurred, with no prior warning to the
people whatsoever.

In the few minutes before the first
waves hit, the sea often receded as
much as 1.6 miles (2.6km), tempting
people out onto the exposed beach.
Some were rather more circumspect,
however. On the Indonesian island of
Simeulue, the memory of an
earthquake tsunami in 1907 was still
alive, so that when the villagers

BELOW: An engraving by Gustave Doré illustrating the phenomenon known as corpse candles or will-o'-the-wisps.

under the macabre name of 'corpse candles', which are said to appear along the paths to cemeteries, warning that a burial is imminent. Wirt Sikes, author of *British Goblins* (1880), collected many eye witness reports of these, one from the passengers of a coach reporting to have seen three corpse candles by a river near Carmarthen in Wales where, a few days later, three men were found drowned.

would break out if sanitation and fresh drinking water were not supplied as soon as possible. The international community responded with US$7 billion in aid.

The economic, social and psychological impacts of the 2004 tsunami were huge, and it is thought that the rebuilding programme will take ten years to complete, with families feeling the consequences of the loss for decades to come. A more positive effect is that a network of tsunami detectors were installed in the Indian Ocean,

starting from November 2005, so that the population would at least have some advance warning if the unspeakable were to occur again.

BALLS OF FIRE

Floating balls of light recur again and again in accounts of the unexpected, variously interpreted as UFOs, spirits of the dead, marsh gas, or ball lightning, and may range in size from a centimetre to a metre in diameter. Fireballs, or floating lights, have also come to be associated with death,

A pseudo-scientific explanation was attempted by Baron Von Reichenbach, who referred to the lights as an 'odic force', which he described as 'a carbonate of ammonium, phosphuretted hydrogen and other products of putrefaction, known and unknown, which liberate odic light in the course of evaporation. When the putrefaction comes to an end, the lights are quenched, the dead have atoned.' (*Letters on Od and Magnetism*, 1926).

A similar explanation has been suggested for will-o'-the-wisps, the balls of light having been seen in other situations as a result of methane arising out of marshes and self-igniting. Other theorists, however, preferred the more poetic explanation that the lights were caused by fairies, differing from the will-o'-the-wisps in being of various colours and, which according to Dermot McManus, *The Middle Kingdom*, 1958, are 'as bright and stable as electric lights'. And, of course, brightly coloured 'fairy lights' are still

RIGHT: An illustration of corpse candles seen in Issay in France in June 1871.

OPPOSITE: Graveyards are places where strange lights are often seen.

RIGHT: Mary Jones (died 1936), a Welsh Methodist revivalist preacher, who attracted strange lights to the Egryn Chapel, near Barmouth, South Wales, in 1904–06. Dozens of witnesses saw the displays, both indoors and out, whenever she preached, and even normally sceptical journalists of the time were impressed. A Daily Mail *reporter described seeing 'a ball of fire 49ft (15m) above the chapel roof. It had a steady, intense yellow brilliance and did not move...Suddenly it disappeared, having lasted a minute-and-a-half...then two lights flashed out, one on each side of the chapel...They shone out brilliantly and steadily for at least 30 seconds'.*

FAR RIGHT: Fireballs and glowing balls of light usually have a scientific explanation.

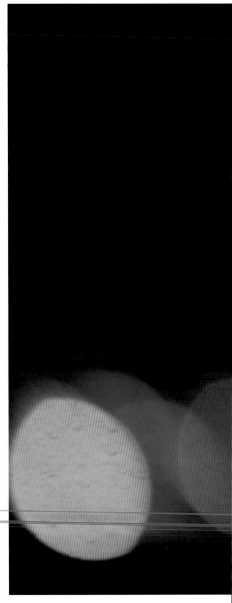

used to decorate Christmas trees during the festive season.

By and large the lights are usually regarded as benign. But opinion is divided where ball lightning is concerned. 'Floating ball lightning is not dangerous to human beings,' declared Professor B.L. Goodlet in the *Journal of the Institute of Electrical Engineers*, July 1937, 'even when it appears in the middle of a group of persons; it appears to avoid them [as] it avoids good conductors.' On the other hand, Frank Lane (*The Elements Rage*, 1945) took the opposite view: 'It is very dangerous to touch a fireball. An inquisitive child once kicked one and thereby caused an explosion which killed eleven cattle and threw the child

the air before disappearing with a loud bang, often accompanied by the smell of ozone, sulphur or nitrogen oxide. It seems to be unaffected by local air currents and gives off little heat before disappearing. But it is somewhat unpredictable: Dr. Neil Charman, of the Manchester Institute of Science and Technology, in an article on the subject in *New Scientist* journal wrote: 'Some lightning balls display an affinity for metal objects and may move along conductors such as wires or metal fences. Others appear within buildings, passing through closed doors and windows with curious ease. Again, chimneys, fireplaces and ovens seem to be favoured haunts for these exotic objects.'

Professor R.C. Jennison, of the University of Kent's electronics

and a companion to the ground.' The oil company, Amoco, certainly has evidence of that, there having been cases of fuel tanker lorries, barges and oil tankers being ignited by ball lightning.

In August 1975 a young housewife in the English Midlands was actually struck by a ball of light that appeared over her cooking stove. She reported it as being about 4in (10cm) across and a bright blue to purple in colour, surrounded by a flaming halo. 'The ball seemed to hit me below the belt, as it

were, and I automatically brushed it away from me and it just disappeared. Where I brushed it away there was a redness and swelling on my left hand. It seemed as if my gold wedding ring was burning into my finger.' The ball also scorched a hole in her skirt, and there was a bang when it disappeared, a phenomenon which other accounts often seem to confirm.

Ball lightning is usually spherical, sometimes pear-shaped or fuzzy at the edges, and comes in a variety of colours. It moves around or hovers in

ABOVE LEFT: The term 'Foo fighter' was used by Allied pilots in the Second World War to describe various unexplained UFOs or mysterious aerial phenomena seen in the skies over Europe and the Pacific theatre.

OPPOSITE: Orbs of light, seen over the Avebury, England, standing stones during the eve of the millennium gathering.

department, would certainly testify to ball lightning's ability to pass through closed doors and, indeed, the metal frame of an aircraft. He was the sole passenger on a flight from New York to Washington, early one morning in March 1963, when he was suddenly awoken by a tremendous crack of lightning. He then saw a glowing sphere, about 8in (20cm) across, emerge from the pilot's cabin. It was a bluish-white in colour, and began to hover down the aisle before disappearing somewhere near the back of the plane.

AURORA BOREALIS

'No pencil can draw it, no colours can paint it, and no words can describe it in all its magnificence.' So wrote a well-known author after seeing the Northern Lights, the fantastic display of visible ultra-violet and infra-red light that occurs in the northern and southernmost latitudes of planet Earth. The Northern Lights are a scientific fact, but their beautiful, shimmering display has been a source of wonder throughout the centuries, even before humankind knew what they really were.

Their scientific name is the *Aurora Borealis*, translating from the Latin as the 'red dawn of the north', which in its way is even more poetic. Although *Aurora Borealis* and Northern Lights are used as generic terms for both, the correct name for them when seen in the southern latitudes are *Aurora Australis* or Southern Lights. Also used are *Aurora Polaris* (Polar Lights) and *Polarlys*, a Norwegian term referring to both the Northern and Southern Lights.

RIGHT & PAGE 190: The Northern Lights, seen in Lappi Finland.

OPPOSITE: The Northern Lights over the Ring of Brodgar, Orkney, Scotland.

The Northern Lights have nothing to do with UFOs or the supernatural, but emanate from the sun. During large solar explosions and flare-ups, quantities of particles are thrown out into deep space, travelling as plasma clouds at up to 600 miles (1000km) per second. It takes them two or three days to reach Earth, even at that speed, when they are caught up in our planet's magnetic field and guided towards the geomagnetic north or south poles. But before they can get there, the solar particles are stopped by the Earth's atmosphere, causing them to collide with atmospheric gases. It is the energy generated during this collision that is emitted as photons, or light particles. There are, of course, many such collisions, and together they add up to the Northern Lights, although 100 million of them are needed before they can be seen with the naked eye.

What colours are seen depends on the height at which the lights originated and the gases involved. The atmosphere consists mainly of nitrogen and oxygen, and a particular gas emits photons of a fixed wavelength. By measuring the wavelength it is possible to identify the different gases in the upper atmosphere. The Northern Lights appear on average 60–70 miles (100–115km) up in the sky, but the strong green light that is visible originates at 75–110 miles up; blue and violet occur mostly below 75 miles, and red can occur from a height of 55–60 miles. Sometimes the lights are seen as entirely red, especially at lower latitudes.

Because the Northern Lights are a result of solar particles being attracted towards the Earth's poles, they are most often seen at these extreme latitudes, and are only seen over the Equator about once in every 200 years. It is not necessary to trek to the North (or South) Pole to see them, however. In Andenes, in northern Norway, the Northern Lights are visible on nearly every dark, clear night at the right time of the year, but down in Oslo, towards the south of the country, they are seen only on three nights a month on average. But travel to northern Scotland and it is possible to see the lights once a month (again, given a clear night), but on the US/Canadian border it might be only twice a year. The lights have even been spotted in Mexico and southern Europe, though this is a once-in-a-decade experience.

The areas where the lights are most often seen, and with the greatest intensity, are known as auroral zones (based on the work of Swiss physicist Herman Fritz in the late 19th century), and later surveys from the ground, rockets and satellites have discovered the zones to be roughly oval in shape. They can be regarded as fixed in space, with reference to the sun, as the Earth revolves beneath it, making for daily variations as to where the lights can be seen. At a point halfway between northern Norway and the archipelago of Svalbard, the lights can be seen at around six in the morning and again 12 hours later.

The strength and thus the visibility of the Northern Lights also depends on solar activity and on the season. With greater solar activity the oval widens and spreads towards the equator, making the lights 20–30 per cent more intense than at times of low solar activity. They are at their most frequent and intense between 10pm and midnight, magnetic time, and in late autumn and early spring. In northern Norway, the lights are best seen in October, February and March. Finally, as the Northern Lights originate from the sun, it follows that they reflect solar cycles as well. Especially brilliant displays can be expected as particularly

active areas of the solar surface come round to face the Earth once in the sun's 27-day rotation cycle. The lights also relate to sunspot activity, which operate on an 11-year cycle.

At their weakest level, the Northern Lights are about as bright as the Milky Way, and at medium strength are brighter than most stars. The most intense displays are as bright as the moon and present a fantastic spectacle, being one of the most awe-inspiring of all the natural phenomena.

DUST DEVILS & WATER SPOUTS

Anyone who has seen the classic 1939 film, *The Wizard of Oz*, will remember the opening sequence, where Dorothy Gale and her dog, Toto, their house and various pieces of farm equipment, are sucked up into the sky by a giant tornado. Dust devils aren't quite as powerful, at least, not on Earth, but they are a spectacular phenomenon nonetheless.

In America's south-west they are also known as dancing devils, to the Navajo Indians they are *chiindii* (meaning ghosts or spirits), while in Death Valley they are sand augers or dust wheels. The Egyptians refer to a

The Navajo Indians refer to dust devils as chiindii, *meaning ghosts or spirits.*

dust devil as a *fasset el 'afreet* (ghost's wind) and it is known to Australia's aborigines as a willy-willy.

Dust devils are rotating updrafts of hot air which, on our planet, rarely get big enough to do serious damage. They have been know to grow to 600ft (1000m) in height, but are usually much smaller, being as little as half a metre across and a few metres tall. It is possible to mistake them for small tornadoes, although dust devils are rather different: while tornadoes come from an updraft attached to clouds in a thunderstorm, dust devils form out of a clear sky.

They form when hot air near the ground rises quickly through a small pocket of cooler, low-pressure air above. Sometimes, their hot air will begin to rotate, sucking in more hot air to replace that rising in the spinning column, at which point the dust devil becomes self-sustaining. The hot air rising will eventually cool and fall back to ground through the centre of the vortex, which helps to keep the whole thing stable. The combination of spinning air and surface friction,

moreover, gives the dust devil its forward motion, and it starts to move across the ground.

Dust devils form most readily on hot, flat, ground under clear skies when the ground has absorbed plenty of solar energy and when there is little wind and a cool atmosphere. When the vortex runs out of hot air to suck in, cooler air is drawn in instead, and the whole structure soon collapses.

LEFT: A dust devil at Haboob, Yemen.

BELOW: Huge dust devils have been observed racing across the surface of the planet Mars.

Terrestial dust devils are rarely large or long-lived enough to cause serious damage, but far bigger ones occur on Mars, up to 50 times as wide and ten times as high, and even then they can

RIGHT & OPPOSITE: The Florida Keys,
where waterspouts occur more frequently
than anywhere else in the world

have a beneficial effect. When a dust
devil passed over MER-A (Mars
Exploration Rover - A), known as *Spirit
Rover*, on Mars, on 12 March 2005, it
had the effect of cleaning the robot's
solar panels and thus greatly increasing
their power levels.

Like dust devils and tornadoes,
waterspouts are vortices reaching up
towards the sky, though in this case
consisting of water as well as air. Most
are weaker than land-based tornadoes
and normally form in moisture-laden
environments, linking the water to a
developing parent cloud or
thunderstorm. Those not associated
with a supercell thunderstorm are 'non-
tornadic' and occur in coastal waters in
tropical and subtropical climates. They
are relatively common (400 a year are
seen in the Florida Keys) and move
slowly, if at all, as their parent cloud is
static, and have wind speeds of less than
67mph (108km/h). Some do occur in
other climates, though they are less
numerous, and about 160 are spotted in
European waters each year.

Tornadic waterspouts, on the other hand, have far more in common with land-based tornadoes, and are formed under mesocyclonic thunderstorms. But they still tend to be weaker than tornadoes, though they can still look spectacular, as water is far heavier than the dust and debris typically carried by them. Although not as strong as a tornado, waterspouts can still be extremely dangerous where shipping, swimmers and even aircraft are concerned.

SUPERCELLS, SPRITES & BLUE JETS

There are thunderstorms and there are supercell thunderstorms. Supercells are the largest, most severe types of thunderstorms occurring on the planet. They can last for hours, though they may be small as well as large, low- as well as high-topped, but whatever the variation lots of hail, torrential rain and strong winds are usually produced, sometimes with strong to violent cyclones as well. The rainfall associated

RIGHT: Storm clouds building up over mountains.

OPPOSITE: Storm clouds containing hail.

with supercells can be truly devastating. Mumbai, in India, was once subjected to an incredible 27.5in (700mm) of rain in only four hours, caused by a supercell cloud formation over 9 miles (15km) up in the atmosphere.

What makes a supercell so intense is its deep rotating updraft or mesocylone, which is formed when a horizontal vortex, caused by wind shear, is turned upright by strong updrafts. If a capping inversion (warm air above cold) develops, this becomes unstable, the supercell developing

LEFT & BELOW: Spectacular bolts of lightning.

rapidly when it weakens. The powerful updraft creates a 'dome' on top of the anvil of the storm, caused by air overshooting the top, while the area directly below the updraft is relatively free from rain, although there may be heavy squalls. The wall cloud is a curious feature resembling a column of cloud descending from the cloud base. Behind this is the precipitation area, where the heavy rain is falling.

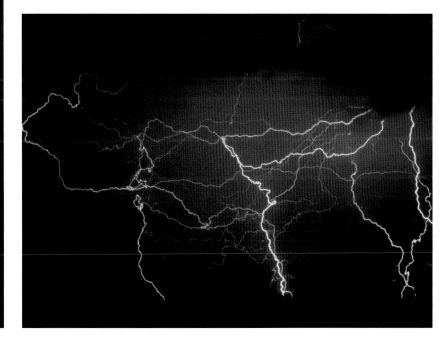

OPPOSITE: A tropical storm over St. Kitts.

BELOW: A storm brewing over Brimstone Hill Fortress, St. Kitts & Nevis.

Low-precipitation, or LP supercells, contain less rain and hail and have a sculpted or corkscrew appearance. Often formed along dry lines, they have little moisture available to them, though they can still produce large hail showers and tornadoes. High-precipitation, or HP supercells, have a much more intense precipitation core that can sometimes surround the mesocyclone, making them especially dangerous, since the tornado inside can be hidden by rain but have a lower potential for severe hail.

Thunderstorms also produce lightning, which not always comes in the form of the classic jagged fork-type, making a break from cloud to ground. At high altitudes, quite different forms of lightning occur. Sprites are seen high up above the stratoform regions of storms, appearing as reddish-orange flashes that last longer than the lightning we know, at a few milliseconds as opposed to 0.1–0.2 milliseconds.

Sprites are triggered by the same transient electric fields as cloud-to-ground lightning but occur a few

milliseconds behind and up to 30 miles (48km) away. They ignite at an altitude of 45–50 miles, showing downward tendrils to about 30 miles and upward ones extending to around 55 miles (88km). They are actually clusters of small balls of ionization 33–330ft (10–100m) across that move downward, followed a few milliseconds later by a separate set moving upwards, both travelling at up to 10 per cent of the speed of light.

The existence of sprites was predicted by a Scottish physicist, C.T.R. Wilson, in the 1920s, but it was not until 1989 that a fast enough camera was able to capture an image. Since then, they have been observed all over the world, and are thought to be a very common feature of large thunderstorm systems. It is thought that sprites may occasionally cause accidents to occur to planes and balloons, and an incident concerning a NASA stratospheric balloon in 1989 was attributed to a sprite. The balloon was flying at a 23-

LEFT: A tornado forming over Avalon, Sydney.

OPPOSITE: Hurricane Gladys, seen from space in 1968.

mile (37-km) altitude above a thunderstorm in Texas when it lost some of its payload. This may have been another type of lightning, however, since the balloon was really too low to have been hit by a sprite.

In fact, a more likely culprit was blue-jet lightning, which projects from the top of a cumulonimbus above a thunderstorm. This often takes the form of a narrow cone, reaching up to an altitude of 25–30 miles. Its blue colour (hence the name) is thought to be due to blue and near-violet emission lines from neutral and ionized molecular nitrogen. Blue jets are far rarer than sprites, and between the first recorded instance in October 1989 and 2007, fewer than 100 images of them were captured. There still remains much of these phenomena to be discovered.

HURRICANES, TYPHOONS & CYCLONES

One of the greatest challenges of the 21st century is to find a source of long-term sustainable energy, large enough to underpin economic development and also be carbon-neutral so as to prevent even more carbon dioxide from entering the atmosphere to increase global warming. Yet vast amounts of

natural energy already exist on our planet, in fact, far more than we can ever use.

Take an average to large hurricane. According to the USA's National Center for Atmospheric Research, one of these produces 70 times more energy in a day than mankind consumes, or

200 times our entire electricity-generating capacity. To put it another way, the amount of energy that actually goes to maintaining the hurricane's spiralling winds is in a huge ratio of 400 to 1. When one considers that there are between 75 and 95 hurricanes each year, our energy problem would appear

to be solved – or would be if we knew how to harness the immense power of these violent storms. But despite being highly destructive, hurricanes also transfer heat and energy from the tropics to temperate latitudes, making them an important part of the Earth's atmospheric circulation and helping to maintain a relatively stable temperature across the planet.

Hurricanes are massive rotating storms, centred around an area of very low pressure. They are only referred to as hurricanes when they occur in the Atlantic. In the Pacific Ocean they are known as typhoons, and in the Indian

LEFT: Hurricane damage at Pinney's Beach on Nevis.

BELOW: A tropical hurricane in full spate.

Ocean as cyclones. But what are they, and how are they able to deliver such prodigious amounts of energy?

Put simply, hurricanes are giant heat engines, relying on a certain combination of temperature, humidity and atmospheric pressure to develop. The process starts as a warm sea heats the air above it. This current of warm, very moist air, rises, creating an area of low pressure on the surface. Colder air

then rushes in towards this low pressure, is warmed, and in turn rises, creating spiralling winds of ever-increasing strength. Eventually, these upward spirals cool at high altitudes, releasing their immense heat and moisture into the atmosphere and forming huge cumulus clouds and rain. The rotation of the Earth causes the rising column to twist, gradually forming a cylinder, or eye, of relatively still air, which the winds whip around at 70mph (113km/h) or more.

Once it gets to this stage, the hurricane becomes stronger by the minute as the rising air heats the atmosphere, causing localized low pressure which further encourages wind to rush up the spiral, which can reach 6 miles (10km) into the sky. But there have to be several specific conditions for this to occur: the sea temperature must be at least 79° F (26° C) to a depth of at least 165ft (50)m, there must be rapid cooling as the air rises, and high humidity in the atmosphere. A high degree of wind shear will prevent the eye from forming.

Hurricane sizes vary, but a 120-mile (195-km) radius is considered small and a 180–360-mile (290–580-km) radius average; only hurricanes 1,000

miles (1600km) across are referred to as very large. Typhoon Tip, to give an extreme example, would have been big enough to have covered nearly half the United States, but fortunately failed to progress that far.

Although hurricanes have immense destructive power on hitting land, this doesn't usually last for very long. The storm's power derives from its ability to suck up vast amounts of moisture into the sky – two billion tons in a day – which is released as rain. Once over dry land, this obviously isn't available and the storm rapidly dissipates. However, it still retains sufficient energy to cause significant damage, as victims of Hurricane Katrina (to take only one example) would confirm.

Katrina was the costliest hurricane of all, in financial terms, and caused damage worth an estimated $100 billion or more while killing over 1,800 people. But even this is dwarfed by the sheer human cost caused by cyclones, especially in the North Indian cyclone basin, where storms tend to hit the densely populated coast. In 1970, the Bhola cyclone killed over 300,000 people, possibly many more, due largely to its powerful storm surge. Typhoon Tip, which occurred in the north-west

The start of a hurricane at Golden Lemon, St. Kitts.

Pacific, was the most intense storm, reaching a minimum pressure of 870mbar and wind speeds of up to 190mph (305km/h).

Although we know the general conditions that cause hurricanes, forecasting them can only happen once they have formed. America now has a sophisticated hurricane warning system, but apart from evacuating people living along the storm's expected path, little can be done to stop them. Experiments in artificially dissipating them proved impractical in the 1950s, due to their sheer size. There was an idea to drop ice into the system, thus reducing the latent heat responsible for driving it.

Finally, current research indicates that global warming may contribute to hurricane development. The number of hurricanes per year has not increased, however, but their intensity has, and this could be partly due to increasingly warmer oceans. It looks as though parts of the world will certainly need those sophisticated warning systems from now on.

FLAMBOYANT NATURE

The Great Barrier Reef

Roving Rocks

The Grand Canyon

The Victoria Falls

CHAPTER EIGHT
FLAMBOYANT NATURE

THE GREAT BARRIER REEF
The Great Barrier Reef, located in the Coral Sea off the coast of Queensland, Australia, is one of the most celebrated tourist destinations in the world. The most extensive coral reef on the planet, it stretches for 1,610 miles (2590km) and covers over 130,000sq miles (336700km²), not all of it underwater. The reef includes 900 islands, 100 of

BELOW, OPPOSITE & PAGES 214–215: Australia's Great Barrier Reef.

which are habitable, with unspoiled rainforest and 2,000 or so plant species.

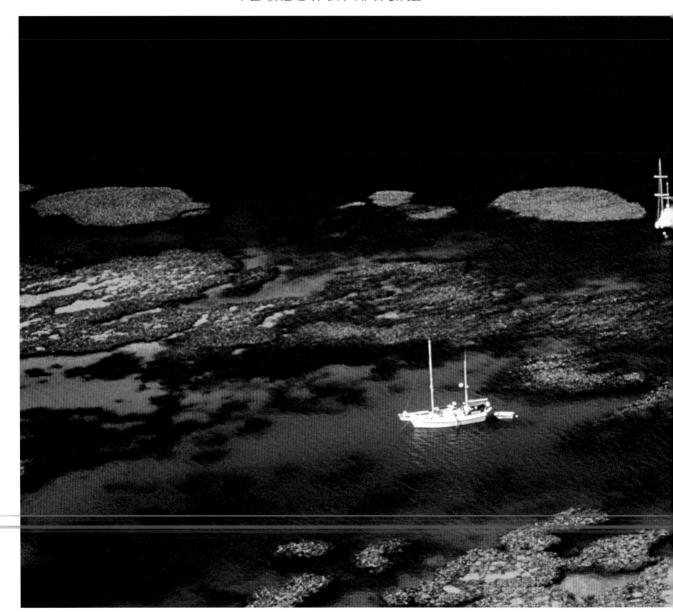

In fact, quite apart from the sheer beauty of the reef's crystal-clear waters and multi-coloured underwater display, one of its most astonishing features is the sheer scale and variety of the wildlife it supports. A look at the list of recorded species gives some idea of the millions of animals, birds and plants that thrive in this environment, including 30 species of whale, dolphin and porpoise alone, with 125 types of shark and stingray.

Six species of sea turtle come here to breed each year, and salt-water crocodiles live in the saltmarshes and mangrove swamps on the Queensland coast. There are sea snakes, and over 1,500 species of fish, including the red-throated emperor (*Lethrinus miniatus*), not to mention 5,000 types of mollusc. It is thought that around 1.5 million birds from over 200 species breed on the island nesting sites, and that there are more than 2,000 species of plants. Little wonder that the Great Barrier Reef is considered to be one of the natural wonders of the world.

Millions of years ago, Australia was located in temperate waters in which it was too cool for coral to grow, but the continent later moved northwards at the rate of 2.75in (7cm)

a year, eventually entering into tropical waters about 25 million years ago. Because of sedimentation, coral was unable to grow off Queensland until about 600,000 years ago, at least on a scale large enough to begin to form a reef. Coral needs particular conditions in which to thrive: it cannot grow above water, or in seas deeper than 490ft (150m), because it needs sunlight, given that it grows vertically from 0.4–6in (1–15cm) a year, spreading horizontally from 1–2cm.

The current reef began growing about 20,000 years ago, when the sea level was about 395ft (120m) lower than it is now, though it rose steadily for the next 14 millennia. As it rose, it allowed the corals to grow on what had been the hills of a coastal plain, which gradually became islands before being submerged beneath the waves of the rising sea. It is the coral on these high points which forms the current reef.

But the bare geological facts of the Great Barrier Reef cannot do justice to the sheer beauty of the place – the underwater coral, the habitats it provides, and the many life forms that thrive in an environment quite unlike anything that exists on land. Besides

the immense variety of life supported by the reef, many endangered species survive here too. Green sea turtles have been recorded, as well as the Indo-Pacific humpback dolphin (*Sousa chinensis*) and the irukandji jellyfish (*Carukia barnesi*). Forty-nine species of pipefish have been seen, also sea snakes that take four years to reach sexual maturity and which have low fertility rates; none of the species found on the reef are endangered, however. On the many islands, birds such as the white-bellied sea eagle (*Haliaeetus leucogaster*) and roseate tern (*Sterna dougallii*) are to be found, while snapper, coral trout and red bass are in abundance, along with over 300 species of ascidian or sea squirt, colourful creatures which attach themselves to rocks and filter out food from the water.

Then there are the corals themselves, both hard and soft species, that breed by mass spawnings during the rising sea temperatures of spring and summer. Hard corals are very similar to sea anemones, but generate a hard skeleton around themselves which is the aragonite material from which the reef itself is composed. Soft corals do not have this calcium carbonate skeleton, but their vivid colours and shapes, like those of the hard corals, help to create the astonishing display of this, the greatest coral reef in the world.

Two million tourists visit the Great Barrier Reef each year; the whole area is carefully managed as the Great Barrier Reef Marine Park, which maintains strong controls over tourism and fishing. But the greatest threat to the reef is neither these nor the run-off pollution from mainland farms, serious though though they may be.

Climate change, and specifically rising sea temperatures, have the potential to destroy or at least cause serious damage, while bleaching occurs when corals expel their symbiotic algae, which effectively kills off the life of the reef. Warmer sea temperatures are known to cause this, and the summer of 2002 saw the worst evidence of damage yet, with between 60 and 95 per cent of individual reefs affected. Not all scientists agree as to how serious this will prove over time, but the Intergovernmental Panel on Climate Change (the authoritative multi-national group of hundreds of scientists) predicts that the reef will

have lost 95 per cent of its living coral by 2050. This is yet more evidence for the urgent need to control climate change to prevent what is potentially an ecological disaster.

ROVING ROCKS

Some of the most frustrating of the strange phenomena are those that we know are occurring but without anyone having witnessed them. Take the moving rocks of Death Valley National Park in California, variously described as roving rocks or wandering rocks, rather as if these lumps of dolomite had minds of their own.

Racetrack Playa is a large, dried-out lake bed in Death Valley, and scattered along it are rocks that move. No one has seen them move, but we know that they do because of the distinctive trails that are left behind in the mud, which is sometimes dry, sometimes oozing, and at certain times of the year flooded to a depth of two or three inches. It is not clear how often the rocks move, or at what speed, and they can weigh anything from a couple of pounds to around 700lb (320kg); what force could possibly have overcome the massive friction involved?

Of course, there have been unlikely theories, such as the ability of these particular rocks to levitate, but scientific opinion holds that freak conditions of wind, ice or mud are enough to get them moving. But although geologists have been studying the rocks for over 50 years, there is still disagreement as to exactly how this strange phenomenon occurs.

John Reid, of Hampshire College in Amherst, Massachusetts, belongs to the ice school of thought, even though it is not a new idea; George M. Stanley first came up with the ice theory in 1955.

Reid believes that on winter nights, when the playa is flooded, thin ice sheets form, locking the rocks in. Then, in the event of a strong wind hitting the ice sheets at a certain angle, they are moved, together with the rocks embedded in them, leaving the rocks still sitting on the slippery mud beneath. When the floodwater drains away and the mud dries out once more, the rocks are left with their tell-tale trails visible behind them.

Reid came to this conclusion after visiting the playa several times between 1987 and 1994. With the help of his students, he boxed in the rocks

he wanted to test on each visit, flooding the area inside the box to simulate the flooded lake bed. Then he and his team attached block-and-tackle and measuring devices to each rock, noting exactly how much force was required to make each one move.

The result? They calculated it would take a 175-mph (280-km) wind (serious hurricane force) to move a 44-lb (20-kg) rock, and a 280-mph (450-kg) force to move a rock of 700lb. Strong winds blow through the valley, but they are not strong enough, leading Reid's team to conclude that wind force alone was not the cause, and that only with the added help of ice sheets could wind do the trick. They also noted that some of the tracks moved in concert, though not quite parallel, as if the rocks that made them were riding in the same moving and rotating ice sheet.

But geologist John Shelton, who published one of the first scientific papers on the Racetrack rocks back in 1953, criticized Reid's findings on the grounds that measurements had been taken on warm days, when the rocks were bogged down in the viscous mud. However, he could envisage freezing temperatures making the rocks move, but in a different way.

The strange natural phenomenon of Racetrack Playa's roving rocks. Here, the tracks left behind by the moving rocks can be clearly seen.

Provided that the playa was rain-soaked, rather than flooded, it could freeze overnight several inches deep into the mud. Next morning, a very thin surface layer of mud would be the first thing to thaw, producing a slippery surface over the still-frozen mud beneath. That, maintained Shelton, would be enough for wind alone to move the rocks, thanks to there being lower friction between the rocks and the mud. He was not dogmatic about this, and accepted that the ice theory could also be true at certain times of the year.

Robert Sharp and Dwight Carey also disputed the ice theory, pointing to some rock tracks that were not congruent at all, but roamed around and sometimes crossed one another's paths. In 1976 they sought to prove the point by planting circles of stakes around certain rocks. When they returned, some of the rocks had moved out of their 'corral', which they could not have done if embedded in a moving sheet of ice.

And so the arguments continue, now with the added sophistication of GPS mapping of the area to give an exact picture of when and whence the rocks move. What is certain is that the roving rocks of Death Valley are no supernatural phenomenon but a natural conundrum still waiting to be solved

THE GRAND CANYON

This a massive gash on the surface of the planet, 277 miles (446km) long, up to 18 miles (29km) wide, and over 1 mile (1.6km) deep. It attracts five million visitors a year and is rightly regarded as one of the natural wonders of the world. Yet the Grand Canyon is not the deepest river gorge in the world. Hell's Canyon, in Idaho, almost equals it, the Cotahusi Canyon in Peru is over 2 miles down at its deepest point, while in the Himalayas there are gorges that are deeper still.

What makes the Grand Canyon special, apart from the stupendous views from both its North and South Rims, is that it has a wonderful story to tell. In geological terms, the canyon is relatively young, created by the Colorado river over six million years, most of it having

The magnificent vista of the Grand Canyon, seen from the North Rim.

FLAMBOYANT NATURE

RIGHT: View from the South Rim.

BELOW: North Rim's Bright Angel Trail.

been carved out during the last two millennia. Consequently, countless strata have been exposed, from the two-billion-year-old Vishnu Schist at the canyon's bottom to the relatively recent 230-million-year-old Kaibab Limestone of the rim. These strata, that would

normally have lain buried beneath billions of tons of rock, are now exposed for all to see, providing a graphic picture of the canyon's geological history. How did this happen?

Most of the Grand Canyon's strata were formed at sea level, deposited in warm, shallow seas and swamps as the sea advanced and retreated. A massive uplift of the Colorado Plateau began about 65 million years ago, pushing the

strata up by 1500–3000m (up to nearly 2 miles). This greatly steepened the gradient of the Colorado river, its tributaries and their equivalents, all that time ago, which naturally increased their speed, force and their ability to cut through rock. The meltwater from Ice Ages meant that more and more water flowed down the Colorado. Then, the Gulf of California opened up 5.3 million years ago, lowering the river's base level and increasing the gradient and cutting action still further, and by 1.2 million years ago the canyon was at its current depth. Not that this was a linear process: the river's erosion varied in speed over the millennia, hence the stepped formations on the canyon sides. About one million years ago volcanic activity spewed ash and lava into the canyon, at times completely blocking the river. Creationists, incidentally, claim that the Grand Canyon was formed by the Great Flood in 2348 BC, which is in contradiction to all the geological evidence.

The canyon walls might seem to be inhospitable, but people have dwelled in caves here since prehistoric times. The Pueblo people, or Anasazi, moved into the canyon and began farming arable patches in about AD 1050, which was a relatively short-lived venture. By 1150, all of the settlements in and around the canyon had been abandoned, probably due to prolonged periods of drought. These people colonized the Four Corners area, as well, with a presence in what is now Utah, Colorado, California and New Mexico. The first Europeans to arrive were the Spanish conquistadors in 1540, though they didn't make it to the base of the canyon. Much later, the US Government sponsored various explorations, including one by Lt. Joseph Ives by way of a steamboat, in an attempt to navigate the area up-river from the Gulf of California. The Ives expedition got as far as the Black Canyon, after two months and 350 miles (565km) of hard going, in which the boat hit a rock and was abandoned.

Today, despite the huge influx of visitors each year, the Grand Canyon is still tough country to explore, and every year many hikers have to be rescued from the base while attempting to walk from rim to river and back up to the opposite rim. They are usually caught out by the climate, underestimating not only how dehydrated they will become but also the temperature difference between the

Angel's Window, North Rim.

rims and the base. The forested rims are high enough for winter snowfalls, with temperatures getting as low as -18° F in winter, while a desert-like heat of over 100° F (38° C) is possible down in the inner gorge. There are sudden localized thunderstorms in late summer, and hikers are discouraged from trying to cross the canyon in a single day; nevertheless, hundreds of fit and experienced hikers continue to make the trip each year.

Having said that, the canyon base is quite accessible, on muleback, by boat or raft as well as on foot. The majority of visitors, however, are content to take in the view from the canyon's rims, where it is like being on a medium-sized mountain, the Southern Rim averaging 6,890ft (2100m) above sea level. For those wishing to experience the scale of the canyon, the Skywalk is the ultimate viewpoint, being a glass-bottomed walkway cantilevered out over the edge of the rim. Commissioned by the Hopi tribe and sited on its reserve, it makes for a spectacular experience, even though it is the subject of controversy: some say this man-made structure has

no place amid the natural magnificence of the Grand Canyon. To minimize intrusiveness, overflights by helicopter and light plane (another popular tourist activity) are now no longer permitted within 1500ft (455m) of each rim edge. As with every important tourist destination, the Grand Canyon needs protecting from its own popularity.

THE VICTORIA FALLS

Mosi-oa-Tunya, the African name for the Victoria Falls, translates as 'the smoke that thunders', which is a fitting description of the 1,000 cubic metres of roaring water that tumbles over a 330-ft (100-m) drop every second. In the rainy season, the spray rises to 2,625ft (800m) and can be seen from 30 miles (50km) away.

Whether or not they qualify as the largest in the world is open to debate. The Victoria Falls, at a maximim drop of 355ft (108m), are certainly taller than the two most comparable in size – Niagara in New York State/Ontario and Iguazu (Brazil/Argentina) – coming somewhere between the two as far as width is concerned, i.e. 5,580ft

RIGHT & PAGE 229: Two views of the spectacular Victoria Falls.

(1700m) against 8,860ft (2700m) for the Iguazu Falls, and have the lowest mean flow rate of all. When one considers how much water per second the Victoria Falls generate, however, they are in a class of their own. They are also thought to be home to the most diverse wildlife, and are classed a UNESCO World Heritage Site.

The Victoria Falls exist thanks to the Zambezi river, which flows along a sheet of nearly flat basalt rock in a shallow valley above the falls; in fact, there are none of the mountains or deep valleys one would normally associate with waterfalls, only a plateau extending for many miles in all directions. Geology readily explains how the falls came to exist: the basalt plateau, which forms the top of the falls, is riven by large cracks filled with softer sandstone rock, the biggest running east–west, with smaller north–south cracks connecting them.

As the softer sandstone erodes more quickly, the river cuts through the north–south connecting cracks until it reaches a large east–west one. When one of these collapses, a new waterfall is formed, the water gushing through the gorges formed by the smaller cracks, which is why the river now zigzags

through a complex of gorges below the current falls. This has been going on for at least 100,000 years, the falls gradually migrating upstream, and it is still going on, the water starting to cut its way back to the next major crack; this will eventually form the new line of the falls.

The actual flow of water depends on the time of year, with a rainy season from late November to early April dramatically increasing the flow to the extent that it is impossible to see the base of the falls, or their face, in the obscuring veil of spray and mist. At the crest of the falls, two wooded islands are big enough not to become flooded, even at this time, but in the dry season the flow stops completely in some areas, making it actually possible for the brave (or foolhardy) to walk along some stretches of the crest at this time of year.

But no one, even in the dry season, would brave the First Gorge, through which the entire flow of the Zambezi is funnelled after tumbling over the falls. Surging into the Second Gorge, the water makes a sharp right turn, where it has carved out a deep pool known as the Boiling Pot, because of its turbulent nature. Debris that is swept over the falls is often found here, including the

bodies of those unfortunate enough to have tumbled over the edge; even a hippo's body once turned up here in this way.

Africans have lived around the falls since the dawn of human history. David Livingstone, the Scottish missionary and explorer, was the first European to see them, in 1855, during his four-year trek from the Upper Zambezi to the sea. 'No one can imagine the beauty of the view from anything witnessed in England,' he wrote. 'It had never been seen before by European eyes; but scenes so lovely must have been gazed upon by angels in their flight.' European settlement began here in 1900, and the falls rapidly became a tourist attraction after the arrival of the railway in 1905.

Today, visitors come for whitewater rafting, kayaking, bungee jumping from the Victoria Bridge and, of course, simply to stand and gaze at this miracle of nature. Unrestricted tourist development is a cause for concern, and political tensions in Zimbabwe have seen visitor numbers slump on that side of the falls. But none of this can detract from a natural phenomenon, that puts mere mortals into perspective in Africa's vast and ancient continent.

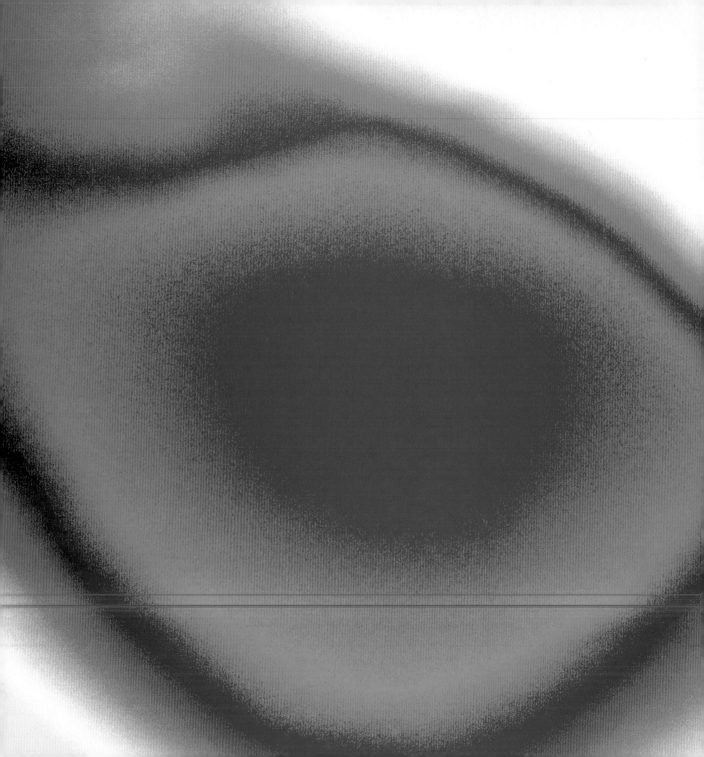

GHOSTLY
GOINGS-ON

CHAPTER NINE
GHOSTLY GOINGS-ON

Have you ever caught sight of something strange and inexplicable out of the corner of your eye? Do you ever get the sense that you are not alone, or that the temperature of your room has suddenly plummeted? Perhaps you are not alone and perhaps, like many thousands of people across the centuries, you are experiencing something that just cannot be explained.

Ghosts have long been associated with hauntings which, according to the

RIGHT: The medium, Eva C., photographed on 8 March 1918 during a séance, with ectoplasm issuing from her facial orifices.

OPPOSITE: Tony O'Rahilly snapped this fire at Wem Town Hall, Shropshire, England, on 19 November 1995, which revealed, when the photograph was developed, what appears to be a ghostly child. Some think there is a connection with a fire that gutted Wem in 1667, caused when a girl accidentally set fire to a thatched roof with a candle.

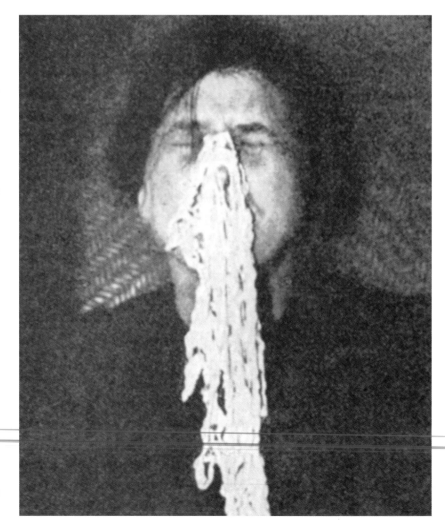

Parapsychological Association, are '...the more or less regular occurrence of paranormal phenomena associated with a particular locality (especially a building) and usually attributed to the activities of a discarnate entity; the phenomena may include apparitions, poltergeist disturbances, cold drafts, sounds of footsteps and voices, and various odours.'

It is widely believed that ghosts are misty, airy, insubstantial forms, which may stem from the earlier idea that a ghost is the spirit of a person that has become separated from their body, much like a person's breath, when exhaling in colder climates, becomes visible as a white mist. This may be the reason why the metaphorical meaning of 'breath' in certain languages, such as the Latin *spiritus* and the Greek *pneuma*, became extended to mean the soul. Although the human soul was sometimes symbolically or literally depicted in ancient cultures as a bird or other animal, it was widely held that it was an exact replica of the body in every feature, even down to the clothing that the person habitually wore. This is depicted in artwork from various ancient cultures, including such works as the Egyptian Book of the Dead,

Hatfield House, in Hertfordshire, was the home for a time of Elizabeth I, before she became Queen of England. It is haunted by a phantom coach and horses, which enters the house and proceeds up the stairs.

which shows deceased people in the afterlife appearing much as they would have done in life.

The former misty transparency of ghostly apparitions may possibly have become translated into the supernatural substance known as ectoplasm, that supposedly exudes from the body of an entranced medium during a séance, and which forms the material from which spirits are able to manifest themselves.

Many think ghosts are shadows from the past, making themselves known to the living, and that events that happened long ago can be repeated in response to unknown triggers. Sometimes apparitions give the impression of being imprisoned in their own time warp, in that they often seem to be unaware of our presence, and do not appear to have noticed that a building associated with them in life has since had doors bricked in, floor levels changed, or has even been moved or demolished.

GHOSTLY GOINGS-ON

FAR LEFT & LEFT: Many famous people, separated by hundreds of years, have been connected with strange manifestations. These include such disparate figures as Anne Boleyn, Henry VIII's tragic queen, and Elvis Presley.

BELOW: This photograph of her children's grave was taken by a mother in around 1947. When developed, it was noticed that an image of a child had appeared, which was of neither of the children who were buried there. No pictures of children had been taken, so a double exposure was out of the question.

OPPOSITE: This picture, a case of double exposure, was taken c.1905 by G.S. Smallwood of Chicago, and shows a girl flanked by two 'spirits'.

Can the thousands of people claiming to have seen ghosts all be wrong? Or are they merely more suggestible than others?

Unexplained presences have been recorded everywhere, although not everyone can claim to have experienced them, and some continue to elude even those professing to be sensitive and attuned to the phenomenon. Ghosts, moreover, do not always fit the

This is the site of a large henge and several stone circles that surround the Wiltshire village of Avebury in England. It is one of the largest and finest of Europe's Neolithic monuments, and is around 5,000 years old.

In 1916, a woman was standing on one of the earthen mounds, looking towards Avebury. Her view, however, was obscured by a village fair, that was currently in progress, in which booths and rides were being enjoyed by many people. The woman watched for a while, but drove off in her car when it started to rain. She later discovered that the last fair to have been held in Avebury was in 1850.

238

STRANGE PHENOMENA

OPPOSITE: Places that have had a long and turbulent history, such as ancient castles, are often connected with ghostly activities, or are those claiming to have observed such phenomena merely letting their imaginations run riot?.

LEFT: The famous Brown Lady of Raynham, photographed on 19 September 1936 at Raynham Hall, Norfolk, England. A man, about to take a picture of the house's interior, was suddenly aware of an indistinct figure moving down the staircase and immediately photographed it. Some, however, believe the image was contrived.

stereotype of the transparent figure, hovering a few inches above the ground. Some manifest themselves as strong and insistent feelings, while others have the power to move physical objects. Very few interact to any great extent with the living, and, if they do, often turn out to be fraudulent.

Are we experiencing time slips? Are we seeing something that is happening elsewhere or which has already happened? Why is it that absent loved ones sometimes see apparitions of relations, only to find that it was at that very moment that the relation died?

Threave Castle, in Dumfriesshire, Scotland, stands on an island in the middle of the River Dee near to Castle Douglas. It was once the stronghold of the infamous Black Douglases, most notably Archibald the Grim. The appeal of visiting the castle is the short trip by boat, when the ferryman is sure to tell his passengers about the castle's ghosts, one of which is a phantom whisperer.

Then there are the classic cases, the ones that continue to intrigue but which no one has ever been able to explain, while most ancient buildings, and even some modern ones, too, still continue to guard their ghostly secrets. But among the tales of historical personages, often connected with power struggles and nefarious deeds, are the more mundane but nevertheless remarkable accounts: the ghosts and apparitions of victims, suicides, murderers and even witches. The term 'ghost' derives from an ancient word meaning guest, so even if we believe in the phenomenon and can

OPPOSITE: This photograph was taken inside Newby Church, near Ripon, North Yorkshire, by the then vicar, Rev. K.F Lord, in the early 1960s. He did not see the ghost when taking the photograph, but it showed up clearly once the film had been developed.

LEFT: The Eiffel Tower, that stands on the Champ de Mars beside the River Seine, is an immense structure of exposed iron latticework supports, which was erected for the Paris Exposition of 1889. Its construction, however, provoked strong reactions from some of the leading figures of the day, such as Émile Zola, Guy de Maupassant and Alexandre Dumas the Younger, who regarded it as monstrous, useless, and an affront to good taste.

It is said that a young man took his girlfriend to the top of the tower with the intention of proposing marriage to her. But she turned him down and he threw her from the tower to her death. Visitors to the tower at night have reported hearing a girl laughing and saying NO, followed by a scream, then silence.

GHOSTLY GOINGS-ON

Exeter Cathedral, in England, is reputed to be haunted by three ghosts: by a nun, who appears during July at around 7.00 pm, but quickly disappears once seen; by a monk, reported as frequenting the area surrounding the cathedral; and most bizarre of all, by a strange apparition which is said to have three heads.

BELOW RIGHT & OPPOSITE:
Graveyards, as well as wooded areas, are
often places where ghostly sightings are
reported.

phenomena, and many of the stories have inevitably done the rounds, having become vastly distorted or embellished over time, while others have been researched to such a degree that a plausible conclusion has been reached in which everything makes sense – barring, of course, the ghost itself.

claim to have experienced it, we should never allow ourselves to become concerned.

There have been many attempts to explain why ghosts appear. Are they the result of intensely emotional conflicts or situations? Are they truly disembodied spirits that have somehow become separated from their mortal remains? Or do they emanate from the realms of our subconscious minds, projected as images for others to see?

Manifestations, moreover, occur in many different forms, from those that could pass for living people to apparitions that appear headless or even worse. It seems that the paranormal can attach itself to inanimate objects, so how can ghostly trains, ships and cars simply be explained away, and what of the plethora of phantom hounds and other such animals that make an appearance from time to time.

A degree of scepticism must inevitably be attached to these

STRANGE PHENOMENA

Durham Castle, in England, was built by the Normans in the 11th century to protect the Bishop of Durham from attack by the English population in the north, who were still resentful and unsettled following the Norman Conquest of England in 1066. It is an excellent example of the early motte-and-bailey castles favoured by the Normans.

The castle is reportedly haunted by the wife of one of the former Prince Bishops of Durham, whose ghost has been seen on the back staircase, down which she is reputed to have fallen and broken her neck.

INDEX

ACKNOWLEDGEMENTS

©ArkReligion.com/Agence Ciric; pages 161, 162-163: ©Art Directors and TRIP Photo Library/Allan Wright; page 242-243: ©Art Directors and TRIP Photo Library/Andria Massey; page 16: ©Art Directors and TRIP Photo Library/Anon; page 121, 201: ©Art Directors and TRIP Photo Library/Bob Turner; pages 21, 194, 199, 206, 245: ©Art Directors and TRIP Photo Library/BR Woods; page 91: ©Art Directors and TRIP Photo Library/Chris Parker; page 207: ©Art Directors and TRIP Photo Library/Chris Rennie; pages 80, 173: ©Art Directors and TRIP Photo Library/Chris Wormald; pages 25, 33, 246-247: ©Art Directors and TRIP Photo Library/Clay Perry; page 108: ©Art Directors and TRIP Photo Library/Colin Gibson; page 30: ©Art Directors and TRIP Photo Library/Constance Toms; pages 27, 31, 59, 68, 200: ©Art Directors and TRIP Photo Library/David Booker; pages 28, 234-235: ©Art Directors and TRIP Photo Library/ David Morgan; pages 97, 213: ©Art Directors and TRIP Photo Library/Don Cole; page 193: ©Art Directors and TRIP Photo Library/Donna Ikenberry; pages 220-221, 223, 225: ©Art Directors and TRIP Photo Library/Douglas Houghton; pages 11, 189, 240: ©Art Directors and TRIP Photo Library/Edward Parker; page 2, 81: ©Art Directors and TRIP Photo Library/ Esther James; pages 90, 94, 238-239: ©Art Directors and TRIP Photo Library/Francoise Pirson; page 133: ©Art Directors and TRIP Photo Library/George Mccarthy; page 60: ©Art Directors and TRIP Photo Library/Gerard Hancock; page 23 below: ©Art Directors and TRIP Photo Library/Helene Rogers; pages 8-9, 11 left, 13, 14, 32, 34, 40-41, 44, 47, 49, 62, 74-75, 76, 78, 88, 100-101, 110-111, 120, 134, 136, 167, 176, 183, 185 202, 203, 209, 210, 230, 250-251: ©Art Directors and TRIP Photo Library/Jack Stanley; page 43: ©Art Directors and TRIP Photo Library/Jane Sweeney; page 61, 85: ©Art Directors and TRIP Photo Library/J Doe; page 212: ©Art Directors and TRIP Photo Library/Jeff Greenberg; pages 196, 197: ©Art Directors and TRIP Photo Library/Jerry Dennis; page 236 top right: ©Art Directors and TRIP Photo Library/Joan Batten; page 174: ©Art Directors and TRIP Photo Library/Joan Wakelin; pages 3, 4, 22, 89, 137, 198: ©Art Directors and TRIP Photo Library/July Drew; pages 82, 83, 84: ©Art Directors and TRIP Photo Library/Martin Barlow; pages 98, 99, 109, 222 left: ©Art Directors and TRIP Photo Library/Mike Feeney; page 131: ©Art Directors and TRIP Photo Library/ Mike Peters; page 5, 26: ©Art Directors and TRIP Photo Library/Nasa; page 195: ©Art Directors and TRIP Photo Library/Norman Price; pages 188, 190: ©Art Directors and TRIP Photo Library/Peter Chadwick; page 64: ©Art Directors and TRIP Photo Library/Peter Matthews; page 103: ©Art Directors and TRIP Photo Library/PL Mitchell; page 92: ©Art Directors and TRIP Photo Library/Robin Nichols; page 73: ©Art Directors and TRIP Photo Library/Robin Smith; pages 14 left, 112, 113, 204, 248: ©Art Directors and TRIP Photo Library/RJ Winstanley Deceased; page 63 ©Art Directors and TRIP Photo Library/Spencer Grant; page 87: ©Art Directors and TRIP Photo Library/Tibor Bognar; pages 66, 77, 226-227, 229, 249: ©Art Directors and TRIP Photo Library/TRIP; page 205: ©Art Directors and TRIP Photo Library/ Victor Kolpakov; page 71: ©Art Directors and TRIP Photo Library/Viestie Collections, Inc. page 218: ©Charles Walker/TopFoto; pages 10 left, 17, 20, 42, 72, 148, 149, 151, 186: ©ClassicStock/TopFoto; page 179: ©DoD at Photri/TopFoto; page 181 top: ©English Heritage/HIP/TopFoto; page 36: ©Fortean/Aarsleff/TopFoto; page 15: ©Fortean/Bord/TopFoto; page 10, 12: ©Fortean/O'Rahilly/TopFoto; page 233: ©Fortean/TopFoto; pages 18 both, 19, 23 top, 35 right, 37, 38, 45, 46 both, 51, 52 both, 53, 54, 55, 65 both, 67, 69 both, 70 left, 104, 105, 122, 123 both, 124 both, 125, 126, 127 all, 128 both, 129, 139, 142, 143, 144, 145, 146, 150 left, 152, 156 right, 157 both, 158 both, 159 both, 160, 181 below, 182, 184 left, 187, 232, 241, 244: © Library of Congress; pages 236 below, 237:©National Pictures/TopFoto; page 50 right: ©Ria/Novosti/TopFoto; pages 116, 117 below: ©Regency House Publishing Ltd. pages; 56, 57, 58: ©Roger-Viollet/TopFoto; page 154: ©TopFoto; pages 24, 117 top, 130, 132: ©TopFoto/AP; page 106, 147:©TopFoto/UPP; page 70 right: ©Topham/Photri; pages 115:©Topham Picturepoint; page 6, 48 both, 50 left, 102, 107, 140, 150 right, 166 left, 168, 169, 170, 171: ©Ullsteinbild/TopFoto; page 11: ©U.S. Navy/TopFoto; page 180.